The **Essential** Buyer's Guide

VOLKSWAGEN
BEETLE

Your marque experts: Richard Copping & Ken Cservenka

T0159523

VELOCE PUBLISHING
THE PUBLISHER OF FINE AUTOMOTIVE BOOKS

Also from Veloce –

Veloce's Essential Buyer's Guide Series
Alfa GT (Booker)
Alfa Romeo Spider Giulia (Booker & Talbott)
Austin Seven (Barker)
BMW GS (Henshaw)
BSA Bantam (Henshaw)
BSA 500 & 650 Twins (Henshaw)
Citroën 2CV (Paxton)
Citroën ID & DS (Heilig)
Corvette C2 1963-1967 (Falconer)
Fiat 500 & 600 (Bobbitt)
Ford Capri (Paxton)
Harley-Davidson Big Twins (Henshaw)
Hinckley Triumph triples & fours 750, 900, 955,
    1000, 1050, 1200 – 1991-2009 (Henshaw)
Honda CBR600 (Henshaw)
Honda FireBlade (Henshaw)
Honda SOHC fours (Henshaw)
Jaguar E-type 3.8 & 4.2-litre (Crespin)
Jaguar E-type V12 5.3-litre (Crespin)
Jaguar XJ 1995-2003 (Crespin)
Jaguar/Daimler XJ6, XJ12 & Sovereign (Crespin)
Jaguar/Daimler XJ40 (Crespin)
Jaguar XJ-S (Crespin)
Jaguar XK8 (Thorley)
Land Rover Series I, II & IIA (Thurman)
MG Midget & A-H Sprite (Horler)
MG TD & TF (Jones)
MGB & MGB GT (Williams)
Mercedes-Benz 280SL-560DSL Roadsters (Bass)
Mercedes-Benz 'Pagoda' 230SL, 250SL & 280SL
    Roadsters & Coupés (Bass)
Mini (Paxton)
Morris Minor & 1000 (Newell)
Norton Commando (Henshaw)
Peugeot 205 GTi (Blackburn)
Porsche 911 SC (Streather)
Porsche 911 (964) (Streather)
Porsche 911 (993) (Streather)
Porsche 911 (996) (Streather)
Porsche 928 (Hemmings)
Rolls-Royce Silver Shadow & Bentley T-Series (Bobbitt)
Subaru Impreza (Hobbs)

Triumph Bonneville (Henshaw)
Triumph Spitfire & GT6 (Baugues)
Triumph Stag (Mort & Fox)
Triumph TR6 (Williams)
Triumph TR7 & TR8 (Williams)
Vespa Scooters (Paxton)
VW Beetle (Cservenka & Copping)
VW Bus (Cservenka & Copping)
VW Golf GTI (Cservenka & Copping)

From Veloce Publishing's new imprints:

Soviet General & field rank officer uniforms: 1955 to
    1991 (Streather)
Soviet military and paramilitary services: female
    uniforms 1941-1991 (Streather)

Complete Dog Massage Manual, The – Gentle Dog
    Care (Robertson)
Dinner with Rover (Paton-Ayre)
Dog Cookies (Schops)
Dog Games – Stimulating play to entertain your dog
    and you (Blenski)
Dog Relax – Relaxed dogs, relaxed owners (Pilguj)
Dogs on wheels (Mort)
Excercising your puppy – a gentle & natural approach
    (Robertson)
Know Your Dog – The guide to a beautiful
    relationship (Birmelin)
Living with an Older Dog (Alderton and Hall)
My dog is blind – but lives life to the full! (Horsky)
Smellorama – nose games for dogs (Theby)
Successful Dog (O'Meara)
Swim to Recovery: The Animal Magic Way (Wong)
Waggy Tails & Wheelchairs (Epp)
Winston ... the dog who changed my life (Klute)
You and Your Border Terrier – The Essential Guide
    (Alderton)
You and Your Cockapoo – The Essential Guide
    (Alderton)

First published in 2005. Reprinted September 2010. Veloce Publishing Ltd., Veloce House, Parkway Farm Business Park, Middle Farm Way, Poundbury, Dorchester, Dorset, DT1 3AR, England. Fax + (0) 1305 250479, e-mail info@veloce.co.uk, web www.veloce.co.uk
ISBN 978-1-904788-72-0/UPC 6-36847-00372-2

Throughout this book logos, model names and designations, etc, have been used for the purposes of identification, illustration and decoration. Such names are the property of the trademark holder as this is not an official publication.
Readers with ideas for automotive books, or books on other transport or related hobby subjects, are invited to write to the editorial director of Veloce Publishing at the above address.

British Library Cataloguing in Publication Data -
A catalogue record for this book is available from the British Library. Typesetting, design and page make-up all by Veloce on Apple Mac. Printed in India by Imprint Digital.

Despite a natural tendency to assume that just about everyone is going to know something about the world's most popular car, particularly when, between us, we've got around 70 years' experience of the model, we've resisted the temptation to miss out the obvious in our attempts to help you find the right Beetle. Remember, too, that just because you've owned a myriad of marques since Adam was a lad, doesn't mean you understand an air-cooled VW.

With such a phenomenal production run, inevitably there are numerous variations of what remains a rigidly air-cooled, insect-shaped auto. Most authors take 60 to 70 thousand words to describe the product. We haven't had that luxury here, however. Instead, we've gone for the overview to ensure that you'll know what age and model of Beetle you are both looking for and at, by the time you've read this book.

This 1960 Beetle is in near concours condition and is one of two cars used for detail shots in the book.

When it comes to our step-by-step inspection of your nominated Beetle, remember that the marks you award, based on our comments, must relate to both age and potential rarity. Mark down a 1946 saloon with dented wings (fenders) and you're in the wrong game. Buy a rotting seventies saloon that will cost more to restore than it can ever be worth and, sadly, you are equally deluded! It's a good idea to refer to the adverts in the specialist magazines, be they dealer or private sale. You'd also be wise to make several visits to the VW shows, where there are always Beetles for sale. As well as concours cars to drool over, you'll find Beetle owners who are invariably happy to give you a value on their own car and offer an opinion on something you might well have your eye on.

One of the last Beetles for the British market and the second car used to illustrate points in this book.

Buying or selling a decent Beetle these days is definitely a question of being in the right place at the right time. We should all be able to steer well clear of the seventies 'basket case' from day one and, by the time you've digested what we've got to say, you should know what contributes to making a particular Beetle a good one.

Ken Cservenka and Richard Copping

Essential Buyer's Guide™ currency

At the time of publication a BG unit of currency "●" equals approximately £1.00/US$2.00/Euro 1.50. Please adjust to suit current exchange rates.

The car that most enthusiasts would like to own, the authors included!

Contents

www.velocebooks.com/www.veloce.co.uk
Details all current books • New book news • Special offers • Newsletter

1 Is it the car for you?
– marriage guidance

Tall and short drivers
VW claimed that two adults of 6ft 7in (2m) could happily occupy the front seats. It's unlikely that anyone would be able to sit in the back at the same time, though!

Weight of controls
No power steering, but even as late as 1978 the steering was described as 'light and sensitive'. The brakes were claimed to be 'extremely' powerful in 1953, but many today would argue that to achieve this, considerable pedal pressure is required.

Will it fit in the garage?
The icon of all small car production will fit into the smallest of garages: the 1303S Beetle, the biggest Beetle, measures 4140mm/13.58ft x 1585mm /5.2ft.

Interior space
Ferdinand Porsche designed the car to carry four adults (an early writer even said there was sufficient headroom for a rear-seat passenger to wear a hat). Rear legroom, however, has been criticized.

Luggage capacity
Later models are better than earlier ones, thanks to several redesigns of the petrol/fuel tank. All cars have additional storage behind the rear seat.
Total capacity:

      1964 torsion bar model: $0.28m^3/10ft^3$

      1971 1302S Beetle: $0.39m^3/14.1ft^3$

Running costs
1968   1200: 37.5mpg/13.27km/litre

          1300: 33.0mpg/11.68km/litre

          1500: 32.0mpg/11.33km/litre

          1500 Semi-automatic: 30.0mpg/10.6km/litre (official VW figures)

Usability
Performance is pedestrian by modern standards, particularly that of the 1200 engine, but there are still sufficient later models about which are practical daily drivers. The front seats are comfortable for the longest journey.

Parts availability
Most items are readily available, but finding parts for a 1950 Standard model might involve an overseas enquiry.

Parts cost
Reasonable, with plenty of aftermarket options. Certain early/rare items will inevitably command premium prices.

Insurance group
About as cheap as you can get! Enthusiasts would recommend an agreed value classic/collector car policy (often with a mileage limitation).

Investment potential
Depending on the model of Beetle selected, you are unlikely to lose out. Pre-1957 cars fetch the highest prices. Seventies Beetles, especially the 1303, aren't quite there yet, and modern/late Mexican Beetles are subject to fairly heavy depreciation for the moment.

Foibles
Know the Beetle and you'll argue that it's near perfect, merely requiring a different driving technique to that of other marques. The uninitiated, however, might refer to 'notorious, sudden, and vicious oversteer', particularly on earlier models.

Plus points
A cult car for many; air-cooled longevity, particularly with the 30 and 34bhp 1200 engine; vulnerable wing (fender) panels simply bolt on, so are easily replaceable.

Minus points
Unusual pedal cluster position; tendency to steam up if quarterlights not used

effectively; heater can be ineffective if non-genuine heat exchangers have been fitted. 6-volt electrics on all cars produced before August 1967 (US market August 1966, 1200 models soldiered on after 1967 with 6-volts).

Alternatives
There's nothing quite like a Beetle. Perhaps VW's Karmann Ghia Coupé (1955 - 1974) could be an option; after all, it's still Beetle underneath, but with a sporty 'designer' body.

Even for the longest journey, comfort is no problem.

2 Cost considerations
– affordable, or a money pit?

VW recommends the following service intervals:
Every 3000 and 6000 miles (4828 and 9656km), or once a year minimum for most lubrication and adjustment cycles, with 30,000 miles (48,279km), or every three years, added for transmission and brake fluid changes.

Small service: ●x60
Large service: ●x150
New clutch: not fitted ●x42-85; fitted ●x155
Rebuilt engine: not fitted ●x1100
Rebuilt gearbox (trans): 1950 ●x500; 1960 ●x450; 1970 ●x420; Auto ●x500
Unleaded cylinder head conversion: not fitted ●x99 Brazil; ●x130 German
Brake calliper each: ●x41 Brazil; ●x65 German
Brake drum: (4 stud) ●x18
Brake disc: ●x22
Brake pad (puck): ●x10-17
Brake shoe: front 53-58; rear 53-68 ●x20
Brake shoe: front 58-79; rear 68-79 ●x10-14
Brake shoe (1302-1303): front ●x25
New front wing (fender): to 1967 ●x64; 1968 on ●x28
New rear wing (fender): from ●x24
New headlight: ●x62-68
Front axle beam: ●x90
Exhaust system (not fitted): ●x35
Steering box: Brazil ●x78; German ●x110
Grooved blade bumper to 1952: ●x250
Blade bumper from 1953: from ●x18; stainless steel ●x95
Europa bumper (1968 on): from ●x20
LHD to RHD conversion (why bother?): from ●x1000
Twin Weber or Dellorto kit to replace original Solex: ●x350
Complete body restoration: from ●x4000
Full re-spray (inc. preparation): from ●x2000
Full professional restoration from basket case: from ●x4000
Body to floorpan seal: ●x15

Parts that are easy to find: Body parts for later cars, service items, most late model trim and seals, engine parts for later cars.

Parts that are hard to find: Transmission parts for semi-automatic, NOS (new old stock) early body and chassis parts, NOS early light units, 25, 30, or early 34bhp engines.

Parts that are very expensive: Early rear lights, early 'W' engine lid, semaphores, early trim and switches.

A new clutch will set you back up to ●x85 if you fit it yourself.

A new headlight will cost up to ●x70.

Few would seriously consider a pre-1967 Beetle as a totally practical mode of daily transport, and even fewer would recommend a pre-August 1957 car as a means of tackling the daily commute. Although the availability of post-1985 Mexican imports has been strictly limited by enthusiast demand, these Beetles, particularly if converted to RHD, will offer sedate but eminently practical motoring for anyone lucky enough to locate one.

1302 and 1303 Beetles have the most generous boots (trunks).

Between August 1967 and the end of German production in January 1978, plus the period from then until 1985 when Volkswagen was importing cars from Mexico to sell to various European markets, there is undoubtedly the makings of a daily driver. However, bear in mind that, while depreciation won't be an issue if polish and Waxoyl are applied liberally, the oldest of these cars are well into middle age.

In heavy urban traffic, or on twisty, hilly country lanes, a 1970 Beetle will get you there just about as quickly as the latest 100bhp-plus showroom offering. Your fuel costs might be a little higher, but your yearly expenditure taking tax, insurance and depreciation into account will certainly be less. However, on decent roads, a modern car will score in every way if getting from A to B in the shortest possible time is your main criteria. The 1600 model, the most powerful Beetle produced after August 1970, offers 0-60 in 18.3 seconds, while the 34bhp 1200 might easily pad that figure out to a yawningly lengthy 32.1 seconds ...

Nowadays, most would-be Beetle owners are looking for a weekend, summer use only, hobby car, and it's at this point that the golden oldies, the six-volters, come to the forefront. It's these cars that gave the Beetle its cult status. The mid-fifties Deluxe model, for example, features superb attention to detail, the most attractive of colour options, graceful curvaceous contours, the silkiest of gearboxes (transmissions) that hardly needs synchromesh on all except first gear, and an engine good

Early cars can carry little more than a spare and toolkit in the luggage compartment.

Semaphores were fitted to all Beetles for far too long! Certainly not practical!

for at least 100,000 miles (160,930km) without any need for major work.

For the masochists out there, the Standard or base model (a rather rare beast these days) offers driving attributes at their most primitive. Apart from the universal and lethal semaphores (until the 1961 model in Europe), these cars have additional inconveniences, such as non-syncromesh transmission, cable brakes, seats fixed with wing nuts, and huge expanses of bare painted metal. However, they are not only great fun to drive once you've mastered the challenge, but also offer their drivers an enormous sense of achievement on each occasion that another epic journey has been successfully accomplished.

For those in the market for a weekend/holiday Beetle, the best option has to be the 1967 model year 1500. Fitted with disc brakes just in case (except in the USA), the car's 1493cc engine offers a combination of torque and sprightly performance other VWs cannot match, while retaining most of the aesthetic attributes of earlier, less well-endowed Beetles.

Although the Beetle was specifically created for four adults in the 'thirties, people have grown larger and, nowadays, even a pair of long-legged 10 year olds exiled to the back seat might complain on a 200 mile (32km) journey. On the other hand, a couple spending a week exploring the countryside, or trundling off to a show, would find their seating firm but comfortable, and would arrive at their destination as calm and stress-free as those using one of today's compact cars.

Although the soft-top, or 'Cabriolet' as it's referred to in VW circles, costs more than the tin-top (a Cabrio owner's jocular insult, not ours) its virtually handcrafted finish guarantees it a special place in the hearts of enthusiasts. Because it's the top of the model range, in later years it benefited from the largest engine option available (except in Italy) and though spartan in comparison to even the smallest of economy saloons today, is likely to have many of the goodies available at the time of original purchase.

Finally, for those whose idea of owning a classic car is the joy of tinkering in the garage, the Beetle's air-cooled engine is simplicity itself, and restoration tends to be easier thanks to that vital combination of bolt-on panels and a separate chassis.

Later cars have wing (fender) mounted flashers.

See Chapter 12 for value assessment. This chapter shows, in percentage terms, the relative value of individual models in **good** condition. Concours (as good or better than new) cars will be worth nearly double, while restoration projects will be worth around a tenth.

1945 – March 1953 – 'Split'

Identifiable by a split rear screen, these cars are theoretically all left-hand drive models. The majority of examples offered for sale are likely to date from mid-1949 onwards when Volkswagen launched the Deluxe model (a more luxuriously trimmed version of the car). The basic Beetle continued in production, becoming known as the Standard. While both cars featured a crash-box (non synchromesh transmission) and cable brakes to start with, the Deluxe model benefited from hydraulic brakes from April 1950. When the car was revamped in October 1952, visually distinguishable by a re-designed dashboard, less delicate more robust bumpers, the provision of quarter-lights in both doors, smaller and chunkier 15in wheels (previously 16in) and a proliferation in

Pre-Oct 1952 Deluxe 'Split'.

Oct 1952-March 1953 Deluxe 'Split.'

bright-work trim on the Deluxe model, synchromesh was introduced on all but first gear (Deluxe model only). All cars were powered by a 25bhp engine. All command a substantial value due to rarity.
100%

March 1953 – July 1957– 'Oval'

From April 1955 North American cars were supplied with front 'fender' mounted bullet-shaped, flashing indicators, sealed beam headlamps and an additional slim bumper rail above the traditional one. Revised larger tail-lights followed in May.

The difference between a late model Split and a first year Oval is the absence of a bar down the rear window. From

1956 'Oval' in Jungle Green.

the end of December 1953, five extra 'horses' were added to the car's engine, while in August 1955 the 'Oval' acquired better rear lights, twin tailpipes, and a redesigned rear valance.

While both cars featured a crash-box (non synchromesh transmission) and cable brakes to start with, the Deluxe model benefited from hydraulic brakes from April 1950. When the car was revamped in October 1952, visually distinguishable by a re-designed dashboard, less delicate more robust

1961 Deluxe in Turquoise.

bumpers, the provision of quarter-lights in both doors, smaller and chunkier 15" wheels (previously 16") and a proliferation in bright-work trim on the Deluxe model, synchromesh was introduced on all but first gear, (Deluxe model only.) All cars were powered by a 25bhp engine.

75%

August 1957 – July 1964

For the 1958 model year, Volkswagen modernised the Beetle dramatically. The rear window size was increased by 95% and the windscreen (windshield) by 17%. The dashboard was totally redesigned.

1965 – bigger windows all round.

From August 1957 North American market cars lost the bullet indicators. These were replaced with tear-drop shaped housings and lenses which were fixed to the top of the 'fender' over and behind the headlights. Semaphore-type direction indicators were retained on all European models until the 1961 model year, and engine output increased to 34bhp on Deluxe cars. Cars of this era will vary wildly in price, with older

1967 1500 – a real driver's car.

examples usually being more expensive.

60%

August 1964 – July 1967

The 1965 year Beetle saw another increase in window size all round. For the first time the windscreen was slightly curved and the wipers parked at the left-hand side.

1968 1300 – first-year with chunky bumpers and vertical headlights.

The following year, August 1965 for the 1966 model year, a 1300cc, 40bhp car was added. In 1966, for the 1967 model year, a 44bhp, 1500cc Beetle with disc brakes became the top model in the range.

US spec 1500 Beetles of 1967 vintage had 12-volt electrics, vertical headlights, and drum brakes.

Price-wise, there is little to distinguish later 6-volt cars from earlier models, although many are prepared to pay a premium for a good 1967, 1500cc Beetle. **50%**

1968 – 1978 Torsion bar models

The 'new' Beetle of 1968 featured 12-volt electrics, vertical headlights, shortened bonnet (hood) and boot (trunk) lids, redesigned valances, and square-section Europa bumpers. The 1200 model remained as before, but a semi-automatic version of the 1500 was added to the range, closely followed by a 1300 version. In 1969 a 1500L and 1300L were added, mainly for domestic consumption. Both cars carried a higher level of trim than standard. Cars destined for America during the 1970 model year were endowed with the single port 1600 engine developed for the Transporter. In 1970 a new type of Beetle was added, and the 1500 disappeared. Models like the 1300A – a basic Beetle but with a bigger engine – emerged, while much larger rear lights appeared in 1974 on every car. For the 1976 model year only the 1200 saloon (and 1600 Cabrio) survived. The 1300 engine as fitted to torsion bar cars from August 1970, '71 model year, had modified cylinder heads

The 1302 Beetle – recognisable by a 'pregnant' front end.

Mexican Beetle – Jubilee model – 1985.

with twin outlet ports. In later life these were regarded as less reliable than the single port engines of old

Prices for vertical headlight Beetles are not as strong as for earlier cars. Limited editions, of which there were more than a handful, might fetch a little premium, depending on their specification, but on the downside, many of the cars for sale are little more than basket cases. **50%**

1302 and 1303 models

The 1302S Beetle, or Super Beetle as it was known in North America, with its 1584cc twin-port engine and MacPherson strut front suspension was launched in August 1970. It shared its double-jointed driveshaft setup with the earlier 1500 Automatic. The 1302S had a much larger boot and reshaped front wings (fenders). Two years later, the 1303 with its 'modern' dashboard and curved windscreen appeared. The 1303 was also the first car to feature much larger rear light clusters.

1302 and 1303 models have a reputation for rust and are held in a lower regard by a proportion of British enthusiasts. Prices are consistently lower than for their 'Torsion Bar' contemporaries.

30%

Mexican Beetles 1978 – 2003

Mexican Beetles were virtually identical to late German models. From 1985, when German imports ceased, the cars were continually developed, ultimately featuring fuel injection, catalytic converters, alarm systems, and colour-coded packages.

Early Mexican Beetles are likely to fetch a similar price to a late German model, or possibly less. There are alarming rumours circulating about the quality of the so-called 'Ultimate Edition'. Beware grossly inflated prices for unregistered, unused cars, and tread cautiously with those that are just a few years old, unless depreciation is not an issue.

30-80%

The Cabriolet Beetle

The hand-finished and, consequently, more expensive softtop (rag-top) was based on the top of the range saloon. Some bright sparks have created their own Cabrios by chopping the roof off a 'normal' car. Avoid such vehicles like the plague, as the genuine item benefits from considerable strengthening to maintain body rigidity. In the UK a lot of left-hand drive examples have been imported: this doesn't affect the prices asked.

American specification 1303-based saloons and Cabriolets came with Bosch fuel injection. Although effective, there was little change to either fuel economy or performance. A catalytic converter was added to California bound cars from August 1974, and remaining US specification cars from August 1976. European owners of US cars tend to prefer Beetles with a carburettor.

A decent Cabrio is likely to set a potential owner back by a considerable amount for an early example, while it's not unusual to see a Concours 1303 go for as much, if not more, than a 'Split' saloon. Comparative rarity and market demand ensure

that even rather ropey seventies Cabrios command a decent figure. Be aware that a Cabrio will cost considerably more than a saloon (sedan) to restore.

75-100% (105% for a concours car)

Concours Cabriolet – the most expensive Beetle!

5 Before you view
– be well informed

Find out as much as possible before viewing the car!

Where is the car?
Inevitably, if a would-be purchaser is searching for a particular model, some of which could be over 50 years old, some travelling might well be necessary. While it's worth taking the gamble to look at a 1953 Standard model with just one previous owner two hundred miles away, it would be wise to set a limit on the distance you'll travel to view a bargain-priced 1303.

Cost of collection and delivery
Unless we are talking about a Beetle that needs a complete restoration, most would-be owners will be eager to collect and drive home their newly acquired purchase (having sorted out insurance, tax, etc.). Again, consider the distance involved, as transport and overnight accommodation are costly. If you have a car 'shipped' to your doorstep, expect a substantial bill.

Dealer or private sale?
While there are a number of firms across the country advertising Beetles, it's unlikely that you'll find one on a main dealer's forecourt. Most 'specialist' firms have premises, but for those that don't and trade from 'home', follow the same basic rule that you would do with a private sale. No assignations in a car park, motorway service station, or some dark and dismal back lane!

Reason for sale?
With a specialist garage, or dealer, the answer is clear, but otherwise it's best to ask! A positive response, for example, of selling to finance another project is fine. However, answers such as 'I always move a car on after six months', or 'I'm selling it for my great grandma who's 103 and has decided to stop driving', might warrant further investigation.

View – when and where?
Yes, how many times have we heard it before? Bought when the light was fading or the rain was teeming down. The simple answer is don't do it! You need to be able to see what the car looks like in daylight, especially the underneath.

LHD to RHD conversion
It's very common in the UK to find late model Mexican Beetles that have been swapped from left- to right-hand drive, and the majority of these have either been carried out by the original supplying 'dealer', or by one or two acknowledged practitioners of the art. If a car has been 're-hooked', find out who did it and check it out with an appropriate expert in a VW club. With so many 'left-hookers' around,

right- to left-hand drive is unheard of. Conversions on earlier models should be avoided, as the car will be devalued by such modification.

Condition
Condition isn't quite as important with a Beetle as it is with some other cars. After all, there's the separate chassis, most body panels are relatively cheap, and having to fit a new engine isn't the end of the world. There are sufficient numbers of Beetles about that you should be able to pick up a reasonable one, and many dating from the fifties are often still very sound propositions.

All original specification?
Finding a Beetle that hasn't even had a dab of paint, if it's not a late model Mexican, could be difficult. However, to crib the sentiments expressed on most concours judging sheets, one restored to a high level is likely to win just as many points, if not more, than a Beetle which remains as the factory despatched it!

Matching numbers?
Identifying the year in which a Beetle was built is easy for, on the car's 'backbone', under the rear seat, is the chassis number. Some books offer an appendix covering chassis numbers, and any reputable club will be able to help. From the 1965 model year, life became easier still, when the first three digits gave a clue to the year (e.g. 118 = 1968 model year). Engine numbers, conveniently stamped to face a casual viewer, tend to be slightly more complicated to interpret, and there's nothing to say that the original will be in place after 30 or 40 years' usage. Again, any club officer should be able to guide the novice on the correct engine type for the year.

Is the seller the legal owner?
Confirm that the person selling the vehicle is both the legal owner and keeper. If not, get the legal owner's details to ensure he/she is aware the car is for sale.

Taxed?
Are road taxes paid so that the car can be used on the public highway? In the UK Beetles built, though not necessarily first registered, before December 31st 1972, are road fund licence exempt, although must still display an 'Historic Vehicle' tax disc: all later 1200 and 1300 Beetles fall into the lower tax band.

Roadworthy?
Most countries have regular, mandatory roadworthiness tests: does the car have a current certificate of roadworthiness (MoT certificate in the UK)? Reams of certificates are a handy guide to the authenticity of a would-be seller's claims about low mileage, or occasional summer use only. A current certificate only acts as a guide to condition when the vehicle was last tested.

Unleaded conversion?
It's been said that VW cylinder heads since the seventies should run happily on

unleaded fuel. Of course, it depends on the origin of the head. When unleaded fuel began to appear VW confused the issue with a leaflet advising one tank full of leaded for every four of unleaded. Fuel-injected Mexican Beetles with catalytic converters must be run on unleaded. Nowadays, most claim that even the oldest Beetles are happy on unleaded. However, additives and genuine leaded fuel are available for the ultra-cautious!

How can you pay?
Dealers tend to be trusting souls who will readily accept a cheque and let you drive off. It's unlikely that many trade vendors will offer a finance deal. Private sellers will want to clear a personal cheque (check) before you drive away, but don't forget the banker's draft (cheque drawn by your bank) option.

Registration/license number?
Confirm the registration/license number of the vehicle so that checks can be made before viewing (see Data checks).

Are you insured to drive if you buy?
There are various sorts of wheezes to ensure temporary cover while you drive your newly purchased 1951 Cabriolet back home, such as adding a Beetle to your daily driver insurance: however, if you have an accident with this cover the car's value will be peanuts according to the insurer. Go for classic car insurance; the prices are reasonable and, above all, you've got an agreed value (you might need to provide photos and an independent valuation from a recognised official of an appropriate club), and there might be an annual mileage restriction.

Auction?
See Auctions section.

Professional vehicle checks
While a number of organisations offer this service, most have a cut-off point of 25 years old. A mobile, qualified engineer will confirm, or otherwise, that the car is mechanically and structurally sound. The service is likely to cost between ●x100 and ●x300.

Data checks
Motoring organisations and specialist companies, such as HPI in the UK, offer data checking services at moderate prices. Checks made include whether the vehicle is recorded as stolen, written off, clocked, plate-changed, or has finance outstanding on it (some guarantee up to ●x10,000 compensation if information is inaccurate).

6 Inspection equipment
– these items will really help

This book
If the authors' combined experience of around 70 years cannot point you in the right direction, what can?

Magnet
Plastic fridge-types are ideal as they're not too strong (and they don't scratch). It's amazing what a chunk of filler can mask. Even a light skim can be costly at a later stage. The magnet reveals all (that is, unless you're buying a car with those remarkably accurate and robust fibreglass wings (fenders) ... or someone unscrupulous has mixed iron filings with the filler).

Torch
Too sunny, and you're dazzled by the bright lights when it comes to looking at a Beetle's hidden corners. Too dull, and you're more than likely to trip over the car and miss its defects. The torch reveals all!

Probe (small screwdriver)
Useful to ease a little mud from a jacking point or under a wing, but don't be surprised if you get flattened if you poke your way into somebody's immaculate bodywork. And if we ever sell a Beetle ... keep your screwdriver away from us!

Reading glasses (if you need them for close work)
What more is there to be said, other than you don't want to pay for something that only vanity led you to buy!

Overalls
Show the seller you mean business. Ideally though, however you dress, don't look too affluent, as that may drive up the price!

Mirror on a stick
Stop ... you won't need this if you crawl under the car, as you should. Beetles have few nooks and crevices, and those that there are won't be visible with a mirror on a stick.

Exterior

There are three areas to make a beeline for when you first examine a Beetle. The first is the sills (rockers), or 'heater channels' as they're known in VW parlance. Look underneath the car behind the running board and check along the panel outboard of the floorpan. Are there any holes? Is it a flat sheet of steel? Is it welded to the floorpan? If the answer to any of these questions is yes, then the car has been bodged, and will cost a king's ransom to put right.

When looking at a Beetle for the first time, it's important to remove your rose-tinted specs and harden your resolve not to buy the first heap of junk that you set eyes on. Paint and bodywork are the most expensive to repair, due to the labour-intensive nature of the procedures involved. With that in mind, you should ask yourself how much of this could you do yourself, or persuade a mate to do with the reward of a few beers at the end of each day? So, you've arrived at the vendor's home and on the drive is this fresh looking, shiny Beetle! Stop, and remember the caution you've just read!

There are three places to make a beeline for when you first see a Beetle. The first is the sills (rockers), or 'heater channels' as they're known in VW parlance. Look underneath the car, behind the running board, and check along the panel outboard of the floorpan. Are there any holes? Has it got pressings in it, or is it a flat sheet of steel? Is it welded to the floorpan? If the answer to any of these questions is yes, then the car has been bodged, and will cost a king's ransom to put right.

A new heater channel, (showing the underside) – a particularly susceptible panel.

Check the heater channel behind the running board, as this often hides the onslaught of the dreaded tin worm. This should be looked at in conjunction with the bottom of the side panel between the rear wing and the door. Examination of the heater channels leads nicely to the jacking point.

No self-respecting Beetle owner would ever jack up their pride and joy using VW's provided points, other than in a dire emergency. Located under the running boards, the area surrounding the jacking point is particularly susceptible to accumulating mud, salt and anything else deposited on the road. In worst case scenarios look out for a running board with a hump - that's where the jacking point has bent up, a symptom of advanced tin worm.

Testing the heater channel for corrosion by squeezing.

Battery location and rear corner; prone to rust, mostly on later models.

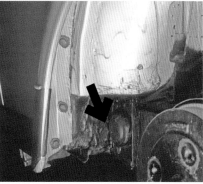

Check under the rear wing (fender) for rust near the torsion bar end.

Look in the area of the front torsion bar tubes, shock absorber tower, and inner wing on post 1968 cars.

If you're satisfied with the underside of the heater channel, open the door and place your thumbs on the outside, just above the running board, and run the ends of your fingers around the channel, just above the floor inside the car. If you squeeze the channel and it gives way with a crackling sound, it will need replacing: walk away and find another car.

If the heater channels are OK, have a look at the floorpans, paying particular attention to the area under the battery. This will often have been replaced with a repair section. Although a competent welder can easily replace the floorpans, you'll also need to employ the services of a paint sprayer.

Having got this far with thumbs up, the second place to look is under the rear seat. Is the corner behind the battery, and its opposite on the left of the car, intact, or is it crumbling away? This tends to be a common problem on post 1968 cars, and usually means that all is not well at the rear end of the heater channels. Confirm your worst fears by looking forward of the rear wheel under the wing (fender).

Lift out the spare wheel and inspect the well.

19

Likewise, look under the wing behind the front wheel to check the condition of the front end of the heater channel. It's also a good idea to check under the wings for badly executed welding. While under the front wing, check the ends of the torsion bar tubes and the shock absorber tower for rust holes, as this is an MoT (roadworthiness) test failure point in the UK. This particularly applies to post 1965 ball-joint steering models. Finally, check under the carpet in the rear luggage area behind the rear seat. This area frequently rusts where the wing meets the floor, often due to the rear windscreen seal leaking.

The third main area to check is under the luggage compartment lid (bonnet/hood). Lift out the spare wheel and check the condition of the well. This area often spoils an otherwise well-restored car.

Interior

Replacement seat covers for later Beetles are readily available. Earlier cars invariably require the services of a competent upholsterer, due to the more varied original seat and trim patterns. Seat condition is, therefore, more important on models built before the mid-sixties.

Watch out for a torn and stained headlining. Pre-1963 cars have a cloth headlining, which costs more to replace than the later plastic versions. Although VW carpets are robust, frayed examples

Some cars have been butchered to receive large, state of the art ICE units!

will be somewhat difficult to restore with accuracy these days. If there's any water swilling around when you lift up the rubber mats, it's another walk away scenario!

Check the dashboard for additional holes, which a previous owner may have made when fitting extra switches, for example. Also, make sure that the radio aperture hasn't been crudely enlarged to fit a bigger radio or stereo, as this is difficult to repair neatly.

Mechanicals

Most suspension components are readily available and affordably priced, except, of course, if you're looking at an early car where the supply of NOS (new old stock) components is drying up. An example of an item rapidly acquiring rarity status would be a 1950s track rod with grease nipples on the ball joints. Exceptions to the 'readily available rule' include torsion bar tubes, which are prone to rusting where the tubes join the upright shock absorber mounts. These should be carefully checked for corrosion as they are relatively expensive and difficult to find prepared for right-hand drive use (though you might come across a used example from a car of a similar vintage). Rusting is more likely to be found on the torsion bar tube design used on post 1965 models.

Next, look under the engine cover (deck-lid). Can you see the road through, or around, the black tinware around the rear of the engine? The rubber seals around the engine, along with the seals surrounding the tubing, play an important role in the prevention of overheating. If they are missing, the heat from the exhaust system is drawn into the engine fan, which is then used to 'cool' the cylinders and heads, resulting in the engine 'frying' itself.

Check all rubber seals, hoses, and covers are present on all models.

Post 1963 cars are fitted with heat exchangers, which are connected to the fan housing with black corrugated hoses, unless some misguided character has fitted the non-standard aluminium hoses which deteriorate rapidly and look horrible! These hoses, or the seals around them, are often missing, along with the pre-heat tube that supplies the carburettor with warm air. The latter should be connected to a metal tube under the rear tinware, adjacent to the exhaust system. Some cars from the late sixties have smaller diameter tubing which exits into the heat exchanger via the front engine plate. Make sure that the seals around the spark plug connectors,

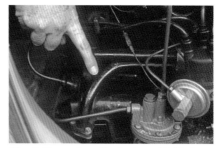

Check the carburettor hot-spot tube for holes and blocking with carbon (will be cold).

which press into the cylinder surrounds, are present and making an airtight seal. If these are missing, or broken, valuable cooling air is lost into the engine bay.

With the engine switched off and the keys away from the ignition, firmly grip the crankshaft pulley that drives the fan belt and attempt to push and pull it. If it moves visibly, the engine is nearing its last gasp, due to wear on the main bearing thrust face beyond normal tolerances (0.004in/0.1mm).

Now is the time to have a quick look for oil leaks. A dribble of oil on one of the strainer plate studs isn't a problem, but lots of oil running down from higher up the engine and dripping off each sump cooling fin could prove to be expensive.

Get the vendor to start the car while you watch the exhaust. A little smoke is normal, especially if the car is parked on a sideways slope. The engine should settle down to a nice even tickover with no smoke. Cars built after 1960 have automatic chokes, which turn off after about two to three minutes. The car should keep running when the choke turns off. However, late model cars with badly worn carburettors, or leaking joints on the three-piece inlet manifold, may stall or be stubborn about running sweetly until the engine is at optimum temperature.

Are there any knocking noises when engine speed increases? This could be due to a variety of reasons, all of which could spell trouble in the future. Ignore slight tappet noises, as a loose tappet is better than a tight and very quiet one on a VW engine.

If all's well you can proceed to a more detailed examination.

Look for rust on door bottoms, rear quarterpanels, heater channels, under crescent-shaped vents (where fitted), and gutters. Check window seals, wheels, tyres, and wings (fenders), and chrome on bumpers.

Look around the headlights, particularly post 1968 models, spare wheel well, torsion bar tube ends, wiring, boot (trunk) lid, window seals, and MacPherson strut tops on 1302/3 models. Also check the brightwork and trim.

Check the bumper mounting points, rear valance, and the wings around the light clusters and their pods. Engine lid and rear window seals are vulnerable. Pre-1968 engine lids are susceptible closest to the handle. Check for rotten exhausts and heat exchangers.

Check the engine for the presence of tinware, hoses and all rubber seals. Check on post 1956 models that engine firewall material is secure. Examine the crankcase and components, and the inside of the lid, for excessive amounts of oil sprayed from the engine. Pay particular attention to engine wiring. Check that the installed engine is correct for the model.

Check headlining and seats for stains and tears, carpets and mats for wear. Lift the mats to check for rust and water (also under the rear seat and in the luggage compartment).

Check all points indicated: 1. Floorpan under the battery; 2. Heater channels; 3. Torsion bar tube uprights; 4. Spare wheel well; 5. Suspension and bumper mounting points under rear wings.

9 Serious evaluation

Circle the Excellent, Good, Average or Poor box of each section as you go along. The totting up procedure is detailed at the end of the chapter. Be realistic in your marking!

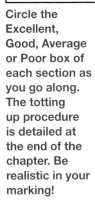

Paint code sticker, behind spare wheel (torsion bar models).

Exterior

Paint

Ex	Gd	Av	Po
4	3	2	1

Unless you're looking at a late model Beetle, you'll be more than lucky to find a car with original VW paint. First of all, check that you're looking at an authentic VW colour (if you are lucky you might find a silver sticker with black lettering indicating both VW's colour terminology and the code), and that there hasn't been a change of colour from the original at some stage. Unless we are talking bare metal resprays, telltale clues about a change of colour can be found inside the vents immediately below the rear window, underneath the dash, and in the boot where all the wiring exists: all might show the original colour. Shade authenticity and changes of colour are only important if points in a concours are a priority.

With resprays there are a number of points to look out for. Does the paintwork look like the skin of an orange? Are there clear signs of runs? Is the paintwork flat, even though there are obvious traces of a recent application of polish? These are all indications that the work wasn't of a sufficiently high standard.

Be particularly wary of a car that has just come out of the paint shop as some vendors will see this as a way of making a quick buck by coughing up a few hundred pounds to hide a myriad of horrors. This is where that magnet might come in useful, for, if glossy hues hide dollops of filler and fibreglass, which in turn might mask something as mind boggling as wads of newspaper, you'll have more than a hint of foul play when the metal doesn't attract the magnet!

Finally on the subject of paint, it's not all that long ago that it was common to see Beetles running around in their original coat of faded, flat paint. Although much scarcer these days, if you do come up against such a beast, don't dismiss it out of hand. It's amazing what a good application of paint restorer and polish can do. However, if you come across a metallic seventies Beetle, beware flat and crazed paint on the roof and bonnet due to the lacquer coat being damaged by sunlight, for it's definitely a full respray job.

Panels

Ex	Gd	Av	Po
4	3	2	1

Here we'll deal with what we can see without opening the boot (trunk) or engine lid, starting from the roof.

It's unusual to find much wrong with the roof of a Beetle,

unless some bright spark has walked across it at some time. The 'gutters' on each side of the roof panel are most vulnerable. Check the seam (where the gutter is folded back onto the main panel) for creeping surface rust and, more importantly, look for crumbling gutters near to the base of the rear window.

Panels around the side windows are generally robust, but check the metalwork below the crescent-shaped vents for paint bubbling.

The vulnerable part of each door is the base, as drainage holes can become blocked, allowing water to build up and rust to form. Also look for crumpled metal close to the prominent hinges. If the car is perfect, apart from one or other of its doors, don't panic, as reasonably priced replacements are readily available for most years.

The rear quarterpanels are notorious for rust near their bases. While the affected area can be cut out and replaced reasonably easily, rust here is invariably symptomatic of more problems behind the running boards.

Gutter – point of corrosion.

Crescent-shaped vent - watch for corrosion below.

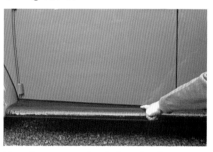

Door bottom ... check that the drain holes on the underside are clear.

Door hinge crease, due to rusty seized hinges, or backing into something with the door open!

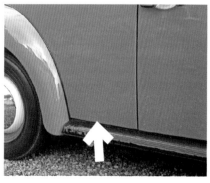

Rear quarter panel.

Pre-1968 engine compartment lids are more vulnerable to rust than later ones, as their design involves a double skin at the point furthest from the lid's hinges, an inevitable weak spot where water collects. The post 1967 product is single-skinned throughout, but two-grille vented lids (1300, 1500, 1302 cars) with protective 'covers' within, might suffer the odd problem, relating once again to trapped water.

As for luggage compartment lids, occasionally, where the metal is folded over to form the lip near the front of the car, splits appear causing annoying, if not terminal, bubbling to the car's paintwork. Much more susceptible to problems is the retaining strip of metal holding the rubber seal between the boot lid and the body (also applicable to engine lids and body). Later Mexican models don't suffer, as the seals are attached directly to the relevant lids.

The rear valance is another vulnerable panel. If buying a pre-1956 Beetle, check that the valance hasn't either been butchered for twin pipes, or fitted with a 1956 or later panel. To replace an early valance will be a relatively costly exercise. Valances from 1956 to 1967 don't usually cause problems, but those fitted from August 1967 are partly doubled-skinned, causing yet another rust trap. After the 1974 model year, the shape of the valance altered again, becoming humped and single-skinned.

The front valance, including the much larger affair on the 1302 and 1303 ranges, tends to last the course, whatever the age of the car. However, beware bubbling and rusting close to the plastic piping sited between the wings and the valance.

As for the wings (fenders) themselves, these are the bits of the Beetle that are

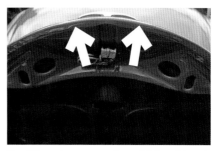

Pre-68 engine compartment lid rust trap!

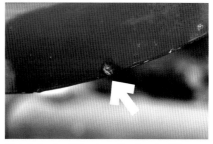

Watch for 'splitting' on the front of the boot (trunk) lid.

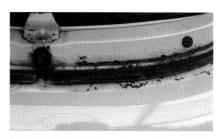

Look out for rust under the lid seals and on the valances.

Rust close to wing (fender) piping.

Vertical headlight rust trap.

The bottom of the rear light pod often rusts. The addition of a side reflector indicates USA specification. (1968 – 1973).

Seam on front quarter panel.

more susceptible than most to parking knocks and scrapes! Fortunately, nearly every year of wing is cheap to replace. Post 1967 cars with vertical headlights have a built-in rust trap below the chrome ring trim, while light fittings attached to the rear wings tend to gather rust at the base if there is a metal surround.

Front quarterpanels, or the metal between the door and the wing, can rust at the base, but it's not common on better Beetles. The seam in front of the door and adjoining the quarterpanel can be problematic, as rust creeps from underneath, and once it's got a hold, it's virtually impossible to cure.

Other rust points

 Ex [4]   Gd [3]   Av [2]   Po [1]

Check under the front wings, paying particular attention to the area where the inner and outer wings meet. Poking and probing here is important and, if the car has already been welded, make sure the job is a good one. Be suspicious if a recent concrete-like coat of underseal has been plastered on!

Next, peer under the rear wings, where the most vulnerable points are the bumper hanger mounts and the area of the inner wing once again closest to the running boards. Large dollops of underseal and weld also need checking.

Shut lines

 Ex [4]   Gd [3]   Av [2]   Po [1]

The gaps around all opening panels should be consistent. Doors do drop through heavy usage causing hinge wear. Check that the door doesn't drop when it's opened, scraping the rubber on the running boards in the process.

Exterior trim

Ex [4] Gd [3] Av [2] Po [1]

Later (plastic) headlight rims and the varying specifications of side panel and bonnet (hood) trims are readily available. OK, perhaps a pre-October 1952 item might be more difficult, but

Bottom edge of front inner wing section.

Section prone to rust under rear wing.

Rear bumper mount.

what oldtimer isn't? The two versions of Wolfsburg Crest bonnet badge, the later offering being simpler, are very collectable, and can fall victim to thieves. However, high quality replicas are readily available.

Chromed bumpers last for generations, unless cheap offerings of Brazilian origin have been substituted. Then you need oodles of chrome polish and never, ever, go out in the rain! NOS (new old stock) bumpers of any vintage (German) are difficult to find, but there are firms offering high quality rechromed products, so a 'nice car' with rotten bumpers isn't the end of the world.

Rust gathers behind the rubber windscreen seal.

	Ex	Gd	Av	Po
Wipers	4	3	2	1

Older blades and arms of any age can be difficult to locate at reasonable prices. Later rubbers aren't as yet a problem. 12-volt cars, except the basic 1200 with plain rounded chromed bumpers or black Europa versions, have two-speed wipers.

	Ex	Gd	Av	Po
Soft top	4	3	2	1

The Cabriolet's soft top is a remarkably robust piece of equipment, but inevitably exposure to the weather over the years takes its toll. New hoods aren't cheap. The specialist club for such cars will be able to help (see 'The Community').

	Ex	Gd	Av	Po
Glass	4	3	2	1

A couple of years ago you could march into your local auto-glass shop and expect availability of glass for a vehicle manufactured before August 1964, but no longer. Window sizes and shapes varied considerably over the years, but it's unusual to buy a Beetle that needs its glass replacing.

Check hood condition – expensive!

	Ex	Gd	Av	Po
Lights	4	3	2	1

Prior to the 1968 model year, all lights were powered by just six-volts, leading to numerous jibes about candles. Tarnished or rusted headlight reflectors will result in diminished light output, but replacements are available.

Rear light housings, particularly those offered from 1961 to the early seventies - two styles - can be nice little rust traps, while really early replacement housings can cost an owner a considerable amount of cash.

All Beetles built before August 1960, except those destined for the US market, featured semaphore indicators. For concours purposes, the addition of later indicators, either front wing mounted flashers or larger housings with indicator bulbs at the rear, will incur severe penalties from a judge. Worse still, should an owner decide to revert to semaphores, near-terminal damage will have been done to the wings.

If it has these, it won't want wing (fender)-mounted flashers too – costly!

Bumper-mounted flashers are vulnerable to knocks.

This type of flasher belongs to 1965 to 1974 models (European specification).

US specification indicator with side/parking light and side reflector from August 1969

Bullet indicators are standard fitment in the USA between April 1955 and July 1957. Sealed beam headlights are also a feature of Beetles destined for the USA.

Wheels and tyres

Ex	Gd	Av	Po
4	3	2	1

Nearly all Beetles, some 1303 models being the exception, were supplied originally with crossply tyres. All Beetle wheels up to the dawning of the seventies had glossy painted wheels, rather than being sprayed silver. Cars from both the fifties and the early sixties are often seen with VW's pleasing combination of two colours.

Tyre condition/rating - wheel condition

Ex	Gd	Av	Po
4	3	2	1

From the start of production until October 1952, Beetles were fitted with 16in x 3in rims shod with 5-00 x 16in crossply tyres. From this point on, the norm was 15in x 4in rims and 5-60 x 15in crossply tyres. A notable exception to this was the 1973, 1303S Big Beetle Special Edition model, which was factory

Five-bolt wheel with crossply tyre ... don't mix with radials ... make sure all hubcap (knaveplate) clips are present.

fitted with 15in x 5¹/₂J rims and 175/70 HR15 radial ply tyres.

From the very early days of radials, owners were fitting the new 155 SR15 Michelin X brand to their Beetles to improve handling and grip, although some would argue that this was achieved at the cost of a little ride comfort.

Until the introduction of the 1500 Beetle in August 1966, all wheels were attached to the hubs using five

Four-bolt wheel.

short bolts. The new car had four bolts. Lesser Beetles soldiered on with the old arrangement, but within a short time even the humble 1200 had been 'upgraded'.

Check that the car has the wheels Wolfsburg intended. If it hasn't, is this what you really want? Check the wheels for damage. Buckled rims may mean that the car has hit the curb, which in turn could have damaged suspension components. Are the wheels rusty, or is there evidence of the wheels having been re-painted? Beetle wheels are notorious for rust damage, and badly pitted ones are difficult to restore to factory standard.

Check that the tyres are all of the same type. A mix and match of makes will lose points in concours and isn't ideal from a safety point of view either. Crucially, ensure that there isn't a lethal mixture of radial and crossply tyres on offer as, apart from anything else, it may be illegal!

Ex Gd Av Po

Hub bearings and steering joints, steering box/rack

With the front of the car safely supported on axle stands, spin the wheels. Hub bearings are usually noisy if worn out. To check for play in the bearings, grip the wheel at the top and bottom and rock it. If there is play, but the bearings aren't noisy, the problem is minor and an adjustment can be easily made. However, if play is present but it's not the wheel bearings, then it's in the kingpin and/ or link pins on early models, or the stub axle swivel joints on later models, which could prove more expensive. On MacPherson strut models this type of play could be the bottom link ball-joint between the strut and the track control arm. Check that the ball-joints on the track rods are free

A typical MacPherson strut as fitted to 1302 and 1303 Super Beetles ('S' models had discs rather than the drum brakes illustrated).

Kingpin steering assembly.

Ball-joint steering assembly.

of excessive play. Vehicle testing stations use a pry bar to check the condition of the various ball-joints, so if you're in any doubt, it might be prudent to enlist the help of your friendly tester.

With the steering in the straight-ahead position, turn the steering wheel left and right. There should be no more than 1 inch (2.54cm) movement before the car's wheels start to move. More than this amount of movement is indicative of

Torsion bar models – remove this plate to reveal steering box adjuster.

a steering box that needs adjustment or, in extreme cases, replacing. 1975 model year 1303 Beetles have a steering rack which should have very little play.

Interior
Seats

	Ex	Gd	Av	Po
	4	3	2	1

The earliest cars featured cloth upholstery as they dated from an age before plastics took hold with a vengeance in countries like Britain. Throughout, North American and home market cars were offered with cloth upholstery and in many instances the more hard-wearing leatherette was only available at extra cost. In the 1970s cloth began to be seen as the fashionable choice everywhere with the result that, with the exception of the Cabriolet which retained wipe-able leatherette for open air and showery motoring, only base model cars in such countries as Britain featured 'plastic' upholstery. Mexican cars, those of post 1978 vintage, featured cloth upholstery in one incarnation or another, until the Beetle's demise in 2003.

A reasonable number of early cars exhibit amazingly well preserved original upholstery, while owners of others have gone to extraordinary lengths to find material of the right texture, type and design, to bring their vintage classic up to spec. 'Ovals', and particularly sixties cars, were kitted out with stylish leatherette, often colour-coded to the car's bodywork.

High mileage Beetles may suffer from stitching coming apart and the odd rip in the material. Worse, replacements incorrect for the year may have been substituted.

From the mid-sixties onwards, basket-weave design leatherette held sway and proved remarkably robust. Watch out for dirty examples of VW's 'pretty' cream option, as this can be

Check the stitching – it rots with age.

difficult to make good. Seventies cloth can be a nightmare. The top of the rear seat backrest appears particularly prone to the power of the sun's rays, and rots with great ease. Up front, the material lifts and separates from the rest of the seat, wrinkling, tearing and becoming a dreadful mess very easily. Amazingly, it appears more difficult to match a seventies cloth than one from the early fifties, while decent re-upholstering costs for all cars are reasonably expensive, there being no distinction between costs for a valuable 'Split' and a run of the mill mid-seventies offering. A word of warning: if the Beetle is fitted with seat covers, insist they're taken off to reveal what lurks beneath ...

Carpets

Beetle carpets were always utilitarian in make-up and sparse in content, as Volkswagen placed more emphasis on hardwearing rubber mats. There were more shades of carpet available in the first two decades of continuous manufacture, but sadly the materials on offer, although attractive, weren't as robust as the achingly dull 'charcoal' weave glued into a typical seventies Beetle. Mexican Beetles, dating from the

Lift the mats to check for damp.

eighties (an age of special offerings) were available with more options once more, most of which were robust.

In some ways it is more important to check the condition of rubber mats and coverings in a Beetle than the carpet, and it's always essential to lift any aftermarket carpet mats to confirm that the original rubber mats haven't been discarded. Worn floor mats from the seventies are easily replaced, but colour-coded mats and 'tunnel' coverings can be a nightmare to find if originality is required.

Headlining

Until the 1963 model year, all Beetle headlinings were made of cloth. Inevitably, few have survived totally intact, and even those that have tend to have darkened with age. The most vulnerable area is where the cloth surrounds the rear window. Replacements are available at a price, although home fitting is a nightmare best avoided. Unless the car desired is particularly rare and there is no choice, avoid one with rotting material, or bodged handiwork to disguise terminal decay. Make sure that a replacement headlining is not only fitted correctly but is also made from the right kind of material in the correct shade for the car.

Once plastic took over from cloth, life became easier, that is unless the car's owner happened to be a smoker. A yellowy colouring or tobacco stains cannot be removed and, while some owners have taken to covering the material with a daub of white emulsion, most enthusiasts couldn't live with this. Headlinings with tears are also terminal cases. Rumour has it that replacements aren't that easy to locate these days, and fitting is just about as difficult as with a cloth offering. From the early seventies, the polka dot punched pattern characteristic of plastic VW headlinings was replaced with plain 'white' padded material, while later Mexican colours varied according to the whim of the design team.

Door cards

Once again, it's a case of the older the car is, the more doubtful the likelihood of finding replacements. Warped door

A warped door card usually signifies damp.

cards, however, can spell trouble in other respects, as they are a reliable sign of water ingress and subsequent blockages.

Door buttons – are they intact?

Door locks

Ex	Gd	Av	Po
4	3	2	1

In a word, robust, although any dodgy character intent on breaking into a Beetle would have little trouble. The small plastic coated pull-up/push-down buttons have proved less tough. However, even when the plastic snaps, it's not impossible to operate the lock with what's left! Locks varied considerably in design over the years, while, as an aside on the security front, it might be worth mentioning that later Mexican Beetles were fitted with an alarm system.

Door handles

Ex	Gd	Av	Po
4	3	2	1

Externally prone to corrosion if not cared for, VW's internal door handles ranged from well made chrome fitments to a series of plastic door pulls. Whatever the age of the car it's unusual to encounter damage.

Door handles – robust and likely to last forever.

Window winders

Ex	Gd	Av	Po
4	3	2	1

Although always nicely executed, window winders have been the curse of many a VW owner. Check that the window winder isn't too stiff in operation and doesn't creak and groan as it carries out its job. Either way, it's a sign that the mechanism contained within the door panel is on its way out, something that will eventually lead to the winder giving up the ghost. Check the quarterlight catches. When VW became security-conscious and fitted chunkier and allegedly thief-proof catches, it also created something that was more failure-prone.

Steering wheel

Ex	Gd	Av	Po
4	3	2	1

The Beetle's steering wheel has had more re-designs than Madonna. All standard wheels are 'massive' in comparison to those fitted to modern day cars. To list all of the numerous variations of wheel fitted over the years wouldn't be practicable, but it's worth noting that specialist firms in the field can refurbish old and, inevitably, rare wheels. Most wheels fitted to Deluxe cars before the mid-sixties were finished in 'ivory', although a few colour-coded examples also exist. Later model German Beetles were fitted with a four-spoke safety wheel.

Recessed door handle – post 1966 models.

Earlier steering wheels can be refurbished ... at a price!

Instrument panel

The Beetle is renowned for the simplicity of its single gauge which contains the tachometer, speedometer, and warning lights for direction indicators, full beam, oil and ignition. Only one basic item was missing (and would be until the 1962 model year) and that was a fuel gauge. When it did finally arrive it was located in its own rectangular-shaped housing (until the 1968 model year). Many owners of earlier cars, dissatisfied with VW's system of a one gallon reserve operated by a tap close to the 'tunnel', fitted an aftermarket gauge, which if included on a car for sale, can be regarded as a positive asset. Similarly, genuine period auxiliary instruments fitted neatly in an appropriate place, can add to the overall value. Conversely, later models so decked out tend to be frowned upon.

No fuel gauge!

Fuel gauge – which finally arrived in 1962.

Handbrake (parking brake)

Ex	Gd	Av	Po
4	3	2	1

All Beetles have a handbrake with separate cables to each rear wheel. If adjusted correctly, it should operate with a maximum of four or five clicks. Earlier cars with a fixed bridge piece on the handbrake lever can still be held on the handbrake to a limited degree if one cable snaps, but with later models and a bridge that swivels all use is lost. If one of the cables is badly adjusted, the swivel type evens out the pull to each wheel. Standard models with cable brakes have a handbrake that works through the same cables and acts on all four wheels.

Engine compartment lining

Ex	Gd	Av	Po
4	3	2	1

While you occasionally hear horror stories of a badly fitted firewall becoming entangled with the Beetle's all-important cooling fan, most have never given trouble. Don't be surprised if an early car lacks what we would regard as essential sound deadening material; such notions didn't materialise until the mid-fifties.

Before 1962, all cars relied on a fuel tap, releasing a one gallon reserve. Basic 1200 models lacked a gauge throughout the rest of the decade.

Luggage compartment interior

Ex	Gd	Av	Po
4	3	2	1

Although luggage space increased, thanks to VW's efforts over the years to redesign the Beetle's luggage compartment-mounted fuel tank, even the very different 1302/3 compartment is not large. Volkswagen never carpeted the area, relying instead on fibreboard to disguise and protect what lay both behind and underneath. Early cards are nigh-on impossible to locate, while later ones have often been replaced with non-original materials. While in the boot (trunk) of a 1302 or 1303, check out the condition of the turrets for the MacPherson struts, as roadworthiness-threatening corrosion can be rife here.

Ex Gd Av Po
4   3   2   1

Lift out the spare wheel and thoroughly check the well. The area is prone to both seam rust and more general corrosion, mainly due to its position on the car and built-in water traps. Make sure that the drainage holes are clear and watch for thick dollops of underseal in this area (a sure sign of disguised decay).

The tool kit in a Beetle, a simple collection of the basics, should be stored in the boot secured in a roll. Until the 1971 model year the jack was located by and fixed to the metalwork within the spare wheel well. Although we have advocated its use only in a dire emergency, it should, nevertheless, be present (the jacks on later cars were stored under the rear seat, adjacent to the battery).

Spare wheel well – with in-built rust traps.

It would be unusual for a seller not to point out the addition of a spare wheel tool kit, for this is a much sought-after and valuable accessory. Expect to pay a small premium for a car so fitted.

Hazet tool kit, suits cars built up to the end of 1965 – expect to pay extra for this.

Jacks on all 6-volt cars and early 12-volt models are located in the boot. (Non-standard washer bottle fitted to this '60 model due to legislation.)

Late model tool kit: often missing. Additionally, all Beetle owners should carry a fan belt and the necessary equipment to fit it.

Mechanicals
Under the bonnet – general impression

Go to the back and lift the engine lid. Is it beautifully clean with everything in place? If the answer is yes, the chances are that it's been well looked after. If you find it covered in oil, plus a black film on the inside of the engine lid, then it's probably been thrashed. There's even a possibility of a broken ring or burnt piston.

With the engine switched off, grip the crankshaft pulley and rock it fore and aft. The movement should be barely perceptible (0.004in/0.01mm). More than this, then the engine has been through the wars and is probably in need of a rebuild. Is the generator/cooling fan drivebelt the correct tension? If not, then chances are it has been slipping, with a resulting loss of cooling air to the engine. This can have serious implications for an air-cooled engine, such as cracked cylinder heads, or cracked/broken pistons and rings. In recent years, there has been a tendency for owners to remove the thermostat and cooling control flaps from the bottom of the fan housing, in the mistaken belief that it will improve the cooling to the cylinders

30bhp engine – simple, but check that the tinware and seals are present.

Early 34bhp engine, same checks as 30bhp – this is the non-fresh air heater box variety.

and heads. The angle of the flaps has been designed to direct most of the air to the hottest part of the engine, which is the cylinder head. The thermostat is there to allow the engine to warm up quickly to its most efficient temperature. To check if the thermostat is in place, look under the right-hand side of the engine between

50bhp engine, twin port, lots of hoses, less accessibility!

The later 34bhp engine was smothered in pipes, bells and whistles!

the crankcase and the heat exchanger or heater box. On pre-1963 cars, the heater control will need to be in the off position, as this opens the rear flaps. On post 1963 cars, there is a two-piece section of tinware that, with the aid of a torch, you must look above to find the thermostat.

In the 15 minute evaluation reference has already been made to the importance of the presence of all engine bay seals, including those around the air hoses, which should also be in good condition to prevent the loss of cooling air, not to mention precious heating air for the interior.

Engine and chassis numbers

Ex Gd Av Po
4 3 2 1

Of the two, the chassis number is the more important in determining the age of the car. The chassis number was stamped into what might best be described as the Beetle's backbone, where the metalwork widens out conveniently under the rear seat. Until 1980, when an international standardised numbering system (VIN) applied to all vehicle manufacturers, VW's system was relatively straightforward. All Beetle chassis numbers began with the figure '1' denoting the first Volkswagen type. Realistically, anyone looking at even the oldest Beetles can expect to find six numbers following on (*e.g.* July 31st 1949 = 1-114 530). By the mid-fifties, an extra digit had appeared, but the type number had been dropped (*e.g.* August 1956 = 1276 742). This system continued until the end of July 1964 and car 1-6 502 399. From August, the model year was added and other figures zeroed at the start of each new year (*e.g.* 115 000 001). From August 1969 the number was permanently extended to 10 digits (*e.g.* 110 2 000 001).

Engine numbers are more complicated still. Throughout production, the number appeared beneath the mounting for the dynamo/alternator. Until the arrival of the 1300 engine, and even when there was a 30bhp and 34bhp engine running side-by-side, dependent on model derivation, numbers simply grew. Yes, the engine's age and whether it corresponds to the month indicated by the chassis number can be worked out, but if the type is correct for the year, or period, it's

The chassis number is located on the backbone of the car under the rear seat.

Engine number (and firing order) under the dynamo/alternator pedestal.

hardly worthwhile. From August 1965, an identifying letter was placed in front of the numbers. 'D' denoted a 34bhp 1200 engine, F the 40bhp 1300 unit (1965 to 1970), H the 44bhp 1500 case (1966 to 1970). AB and AR referred to 44bhp 1300 twin-port head engines from 1970 to 1973 and 1973 to 1975 respectively.

AD and AS denoted the 1600 twin-port head engine, the former allocated to the 50bhp offering from 1970 to 1973, and the latter from 1973 until the last Cabriolet rolled out of the Karmann plant in 1980. If an 'X' or two arrows pointing in opposite directions appear before the engine number, this indicates a genuine replacement factory unit.

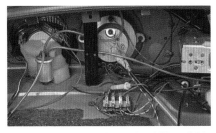

Ideally, even early wiring should be of this standard.

Simple wiring but in good nick!

Wiring

Ex 4 Gd 3 Av 2 Po 1

While under the luggage compartment lid have a good look at the wiring which, on Torsion Bar cars, is conveniently situated behind the dashboard, and is accessed from a removable fibreboard panel under the bonnet. Are there lots of crimped insulated spade connectors with gaudy red, blue or yellow insulation? This usually indicates trouble, especially if accompanied by a rat's nest of non-standard wiring colours. Worse still, you may find 'Scotch-loc' style connectors. These are OK as a temporary repair to get you home, but can give trouble if used long term.

There are surprisingly few wires

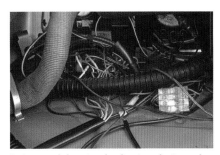

Later models, standard setup, but much more of a rat's nest.

in the engine bay but, due to the heat and presence of oil, the insulation often becomes brittle. Particularly prone to this problem is the important wire from the oil pressure warning switch. On cars built during the sixties and beyond, check that the black wire from the coil to the automatic choke element, via the cut-off valve on the carburettor, is present and in good condition. Early Beetles have the voltage regulator mounted on the generator in the engine bay; on later cars it's mounted under the left rear seat. Make sure that the connections to the regulator are tight and corrosion-free. Later cars have the main wiring loom from front to back running along the inside edge of the left-hand heater channel. Check that the insulation on this has not been damaged, especially if the heater channel has been welded.

Battery

Ex	Gd	Av	Po
4	3	2	1

The battery is mounted under the right-hand rear seat and, on early cars, has an insulated metal cover held down with a strap. Later Beetles have a battery with recessed terminals and should have a plastic flap (often missing) over the positive terminal. The covers and hold down strap are important to stop the seat springs shorting the battery and causing a fire. If there is a lot of corrosion on the terminals then the battery is probably past its best. Beware the owner who charges the battery before you arrive!

6-volt battery – make sure the cover is in place and serviceable.

12-volt battery has recessed terminals ... ideally, the live terminal is covered with a plastic flap, as here.

Windscreen washer system

Ex	Gd	Av	Po
4	3	2	1

Windscreen washers were factory fitted from August 1960, and operated by a push switch in the centre of the windscreen wiper switch on the right-hand side of the centre of the dashboard. 1960 systems were pressurised by a hand pump on the instrument panel. A washer bottle incorporating a tyre valve, which could be pressurised at the same time as the tyres were pumped up, followed this design in 1961. In 1970, the bottle was pressurised by fitting a connection to the spare wheel. This system is very simple and only fails through loss of compressed air. The bottle holds about one litre and is situated behind the spare wheel in the front luggage compartment. From August 1967, the washer bottle was located in the spare wheel by two lugs through the wheel boltholes, and held in place by two pegs. On 1302 and 1303 models the bottle is located at the front right-hand side of the boot. From 1982, Mexican-built cars were fitted with electric windscreen washers.

Later German washer bottles used compressed air from the spare tyre.

1302 and 1303 washer bottles were attached to the right-hand side of the boot (trunk), but still worked on tyre pressure.

Engine leaks

Ex Gd Av Po
4 3 2 1

Have a good look above and below the engine. Is it plastered with oil and muck? Remove the oil filler cap and check for buff/creamy gunge. These are both signs of a well-worn engine. Spilt oil at the top of the engine could be due to insufficient care being taken when topping up, or the black tinware surrounding the oil filler tube being loose or rusted through, thanks to water in the aforementioned creamy gunge. It could also be due to perished oil cooler seals, or worn pistons and piston rings causing the crankcase to pressurise, resulting in oil blowing out of every available orifice. Looking underneath, oil at the front of the engine, where it joins the transmission, is usually from the crankshaft oil seal, although it could be from the gearbox shaft seal. Gearbox oil has a very strong smell. Oil along the right-hand side of the engine is either the valve cover gasket or the pushrod tube oil seals leaking. Check this with a torch, looking above the tinware between the heat exchanger and the crankcase. Check in the same place for the thermostat as this has often been removed (a definite no-no). Also check the left-hand side for the same leaks, and look above the pushrod tubes for oil. If you find oil here it could be the oil cooler and/or pushrod tube seals again, but it could also be a cracked crankcase. This is a terminal condition, requiring a complete engine rebuild using a replacement crankcase.

Engine mountings

Ex Gd Av Po
4 3 2 1

As the engine hangs off the rear of the gearbox there are no engine mountings as such. The gearbox is mounted between the rear floorpan forks on a metal cradle. You can visually check the rubber mountings between the cradle and the gearbox to see if they have been affected by oil, but they rarely give any trouble. The third mounting point is at the front of the gearbox and, again, can only be visually inspected. This is better done with the car on a ramp, as you can then try to move the front of the gearbox up and down to check if the mount is sound.

Intake manifold

Ex Gd Av Po
4 3 2 1

The carburettor to inlet manifold gasket on post 1971 engines, plus the metal ring between the manifold and the cylinder heads, should be in good condition to prevent air leaks. Air ingress into the inlet manifold causes a weakening of the fuel/air mixture and a loss of smooth running. The problem can be detected by listening for a hissing noise.

The handlebar type manifold used on pre-1971 engines rarely gives any trouble in itself, but the attached pre-heat pipe can either rust through, or become blocked with carbon. Visually inspect the pre-heat pipe and then, with the engine running, check if it warms up.

Inlet manifold, showing carburettor 'hot-spot' tube.

Be very careful, as this pipe can get very hot if it's working correctly (as a precaution, check for warmth near the centre under the carburettor). A consequence of this pipe being blocked is that the upright part of the manifold can ice-up during winter, causing rough running.

Post 1971 engines of 1300cc or more have twin-port heads and a three-piece inlet manifold. In addition to the checks already made, there are two rubber joints which are held in place by hose clips; these can perish and cause a weakening of the fuel mixture.

Carburettors/fuel injection system

Ex	Gd	Av	Po
4	3	2	1

Early carburettors are less troublesome than those used on later cars which, thanks to anti-pollution legislation, have been made more complicated. The main throttle spindle can become sloppy, causing air leaks and a small loss of fuel, the result of which will be poor running. Try to rock the spindle back and forth to check this.

Due to wear and tear, a lot of Beetle carburettors have been replaced. Consequently, it's not unusual to find a car fitted with a Weber carburettor, which is fine except for the finicky concours judge. Sadly, others have copies of the original Solex from dubious origins, which can be troublesome, thanks to poor workmanship during manufacture. There is at least one company rebuilding original Solex carbs, complete with new throttle spindle bearings, and these are a better bet.

Late model carbs are more complex than earlier models.

There are a few seventies US market Beetles, invariably Cabriolets, in Britain that had a complicated fuel injection system which has proved troublesome. Late model Mexican-built cars have less complicated fuel injection systems which, to date, have proved reliable.

Exhaust

Ex	Gd	Av	Po
4	3	2	1

The best and most efficient exhaust systems are the types fitted by the factory. Many cars are now fitted with go-faster aftermarket extractor systems, which cause complications with the heating system, as they lack the transfer pods for the heater tubes from the fan housing. Additionally, their pipework might be so close to the rear valance that it blisters the paint, and, when failure

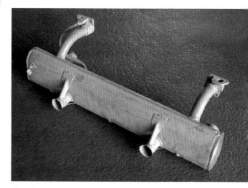

Don't worry if the exhaust has expired; it's cheap and easy to replace!

occurs, they could burn through the mudflaps, if fitted!

Beetle exhaust systems rarely last more than two years if the car is in continuous use. An exhaust is relatively cheap to buy if made by the original equipment manufacturer, and then purchased from an independent trader. Inevitably, exhausts for both 25 and 30bhp engines are more difficult to source and will cost more, but the fact that an otherwise excellent car has a 'dodgy' exhaust shouldn't deter a potential purchaser. Original-type exhausts usually fail near the seam on the ends of the main box.

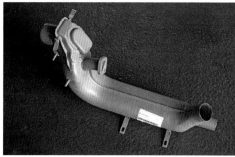

Heat exchanger: a relatively expensive universal reproduction part for Beetles/ some Transporters. Exhaust gasses from cylinders one and three pass through these *en route* to the exhaust box.

Gearbox (transmission), rear axle and clutch

Ex	Gd	Av	Po
4	3	2	1

Beetle drivelines, especially on early cars, are relatively trouble-free, with even noisy examples going on for years before anything breaks. Sometimes, you'll find a car that slips out of gear, but this is rare. Transmission noise is usually from the final drive (crownwheel and pinion). The usual problems are driveshaft related, with swing axles having leaky driveshaft gaiters and double-jointed driveshafts suffering from worn constant velocity joints or split joint gaiters. Visually check the swing axle gaiters, or constant velocity joint gaiters, for splits. Badly worn constant velocity joints click (mainly) when cornering.

Semi-automatic models have a manual gearbox mated to a servo-operated clutch and a torque converter. They rarely give trouble; the oil seal on the torque converter occasionally requires replacing. Infrequently, these models can suffer from clutch slip, which is most likely to be caused by contamination via a leaky oil seal into the dry area of the gearbox where the clutch is situated.

On manual cars, clutch free play at the pedal should be 10-20mm.

Test drive (not less than 15 minutes)
Main warning lights (telltales)

Ex	Gd	Av	Po
4	3	2	1

There are two warning lights situated in the speedometer head which are important for the health of the engine; the red generator warning light and the green oil pressure warning light. On some earlier models, and then again with later ones, both lights are red. When the engine starts both lights should extinguish. On cars with very good oil pressure the green warning light may stay on for a few seconds after the engine is switched off as long as the ignition is still on.

Cold start

Ex	Gd	Av	Po
4	3	2	1

On cars built before August 1960, pull out the manual choke. For later models, press the accelerator pedal once to activate the automatic choke, then, with your foot off the accelerator pedal, turn the starter key; the vehicle should start if it has been correctly maintained.

Ex	Gd	Av	Po
4	3	2	1

Clutch operation

The clutch pedal, which should have 10 – 20mm of free play before you can feel the spring pressure, can now be depressed and the gearlever should slip smoothly into first. On releasing the clutch it should not judder. A juddering clutch can be due to three reasons: oil on the driven plate, not enough curve in the conduit between the chassis and the bracket on the gearbox, or simply that the clutch is nearing the end of its life.

Ex	Gd	Av	Po
4	3	2	1

Gearbox (transmission) operation (including reverse)

Early cars had no synchromesh on first gear, and Standard models had a crash-box which required the driver to double de-clutch when changing gear. All other Beetles had full synchromesh and, if in good condition, a very smooth action. When testing, drive the car fairly hard in each gear, making sure that it doesn't jump out of any of them. Test reverse in this way somewhere quiet, like an empty car park. Find reverse by pushing down on the lever, which is then moved to the left and back.

Ex	Gd	Av	Po
4	3	2	1

Auto box operation

The 'automatic' Beetle is in fact a semi-automatic, and the system operates in the following way. The gearbox is a three-speed unit built in the same way as the manual version, but without first gear. The gears are changed via a lever assisted by a servo-operated clutch. A torque converter smoothes out the acceleration and also allows the car to be driven in top gear like a full automatic. The starter will not operate if a gear is selected.

When the gearlever (shiftlever) is depressed, a contact at the bottom of the lever stimulates a solenoid in the engine compartment. This controls a valve which, in turn, activates the servo-operated clutch lever. This allows smooth passage into each gear position. The car can, therefore, be driven like a clutch pedal-free manual, or a full automatic by using top gear only and allowing the torque converter to slip during acceleration.

Faults include a leaking torque converter oil seal and a slipping clutch. Parts are now hard to find for this model, but there are still specialists who can repair the gearbox.

Ex	Gd	Av	Po
4	3	2	1

Steering feel

Although heavy at slow speeds compared to modern power-assisted cars, the steering should feel light and positive once on the move. The general tendency is towards over-steer and the most stable technique is to approach a bend at a speed where you can gently accelerate through it.

Lowered cars usually feel awful, as they often feature adjusting devices let into the front torsion bars which alter the steering geometry (the best way to lower a Beetle is to use drop-spindles, where the stub-axles are located higher up the axle assembly and the steering geometry remains the same as standard).

Brake operation (including handbrake/parking brake)

Ex 4 Gd 3 Av 2 Po 1

Disc brakes are best as they pull up in a straight line (unless a calliper is seized). If drum brakes are adjusted correctly, they work satisfactorily, but often have a tendency to pull toward the gutter due to the camber of the road (1200cc Beetles built in 1970 had a bad reputation for this problem). If you can feel a slight pulsing through the pedal when you brake, the car has distorted drums or discs. The handbrake, if adjusted correctly to about four or five clicks, is a very capable device, able to hold the car on quite steep hills.

Noises

Ex 4 Gd 3 Av 2 Po 1

Although these will be hard to define, here are a few personal experiences. A broken crankshaft, most common with 30bhp Beetles, can be quiet at a certain speed, but make an awful noise when travelling faster or slower. A broken piston makes a '*chang chang*' sound, while with a failed valve spring there's a '*tak tak*' sound. A scraping sound from the front, when cornering at town speeds, is often due to badly adjusted front wheel bearings, causing the front brakes to rub. A low rumble from the back end can be due to a worn rear wheel bearing. Cars with the double-jointed driveshafts '*click*' when cornering if a constant velocity joint is about to fail. Most older Beetles suffer from a bit of gearbox/transmission whine, and this is particularly true of cars with the crash-box.

Oil pressure

Ex 4 Gd 3 Av 2 Po 1

If the oil pressure warning light comes on when driving, stop immediately and check the oil level, as the light only comes on when there is hardly any oil pressure left. A healthy Beetle operates at 28psi maximum, although there is no way of checking this with the standard setup. Gauges are available from VDO, but they do make you paranoid!

Charging rate

Ex 4 Gd 3 Av 2 Po 1

As long as the generator warning light stays off when driving, you can assume that it's charging OK. If the warning light comes on when driving, stop immediately! You may have a broken fan belt (which has serious consequences for the health of the engine). The charging rate can be checked using a multimeter, using the techniques outlined in a good workshop manual.

Controls operation

Ex 4 Gd 3 Av 2 Po 1

Apart from the pedals standing upright with the pivot at floor level, all the major controls are similar to most makes of cars of the era. A rotating knob adjacent to the handbrake lever on early models controls the heater. Later models have a pull up lever on the right to control heater output. Additionally, later cars have a lever on the left of the handbrake to regulate the heat to the rear footwell. Beetles built before October 1952 were fitted with a choke control knob on the transmission tunnel, which then moved to the dashboard for models built until July 1960.

Operation switches

Ex 4 Gd 3 Av 2 Po 1

The Beetle is renowned for its simple yet functional dashboard.

Very early models until October 1952 were fitted with two turn switches to control the lights and wipers, while an additional switch in the centre of the dashboard controlled the semaphore indicators. Pull switches appeared after October 1952 until July 1966, along with a stalk on the steering column to control the indicators. In August 1967, the lights and wipers controls reverted to rotary switches. August 1967 saw the introduction of two additional switches to control the fresh air ventilation and another to control the hazard warning lights. In August 1971, with the introduction of the four-spoke safety steering wheel, the wiper switch became a stalk on the right-hand side of the column. 1303 Beetles have rocker switches to operate lights, hazard warning lights and the heated rear screen.

Ramp check

Your local tyre/exhaust depot should allow you to raise the car on a ramp for a better inspection of the underside.

Inspect flexible brake pipes for cracking and/or bulging while your assistant presses the brake pedal. Check all the metal brake pipes for corrosion and signs of leakage. Have your assistant rock the steering wheel while set straight ahead, and then in both full lock positions. While the steering is being rocked, check the steering track-rod ball-joints, steering-box and steering-swivel ball-joints for excessive play (lash).

Check the floorpan for corrosion, paying particular attention to where the front frame head joins the tunnel. The area under the battery is also prone to corrosion. Check the underside of the heater channels (sills/rockers) for corrosion, and that there hasn't been a bodge done by fitting a plate underneath and welding it to the floorpan.

The underside of the fuel tank is best inspected with a front wheel removed, but can be seen from under the car with a little effort. The rigid fuel pipe runs through the tunnel and is connected at each end with flexible tubing, which should be secured by suitable clips. Failure of these flexible pipes, or a lack of hose clips, results in barbecued Beetles ...

Check for engine and transmission oil leaks. Pay attention to the rubber axle boots on swing axle cars and the driveshaft gaiters on the double-jointed axle models. Inspect the exhaust box as it has a fairly limited lifespan, but it's cheap compared to most cars and fairly easy to fit. Note that heat exchangers are relatively expensive.

Evaluation procedure

Add up the total points score: **196 = excellent, possibly concours; 147 = good; 98 = average; 49 = poor**. Cars scoring over 130 will be completely useable and will require only maintenance and care to keep in condition. Cars scoring between 49 and 100 will require full restoration (at much the same cost), cars scoring between 101 and 129 will require very careful assesment of necessary repair/restoration costs in order to reach a realistic value.

10 Auctions
– sold! Another way to buy your dream

Auction pros and cons

Pros: Prices will usually be lower than those of dealers or private sellers, and you might grab a real bargain on the day. Auctioneers have usually established clear title with the seller.

Cons: You have to rely on a sketchy catalogue description of condition and history. The opportunity to inspect is limited and you cannot drive the car. Auction cars are often a little below par and may require some work.

Which auction?

Auctions are advertised in car magazines and on the auction houses' websites. A catalogue, or a simple printed list of the lots for auction, might only be available a day or two ahead, though often lots are listed and pictured on auctioneers' websites much earlier. Contact the auction company to ask if previous auction selling prices are available as this is useful information (details of past sales are often available on websites).

Catalogue, entry fee and payment details

When you purchase the catalogue of the vehicles in the auction, it often acts as a ticket allowing two people to attend the viewing days and the auction. Catalogue details tend to be comparatively brief, but will include information such as 'one owner from new, low mileage, full service history', etc. It will also usually show a guide price to give you some idea of what to expect to pay and will tell you what is charged as a 'Buyer's premium'. The catalogue will also contain details of acceptable forms of payment. At the fall of the hammer an immediate deposit is usually required, the balance payable within 24 hours. If the plan is to pay by cash there may be a cash limit. Some auctions will accept payment by debit card. Sometimes credit or charge cards are acceptable, but will often incur an extra charge. A bank draft or bank transfer will have to be arranged in advance with your own bank as well as with the auction house. No car will be released before **all** payments are cleared. If delays occur in payment transfers then storage costs can accrue.

Buyer's premium

A buyer's premium will be added to the hammer price: **don't** forget this in your calculations. It's not usual for there to be a further state tax or local tax on the purchase price and/or on the buyer's premium.

Viewing

In some instances it's possible to view on the day, or days before, as well as in the hours prior to, the auction. There are auction officials available who are willing to help out by opening engine and luggage compartments and to allow you to inspect the interior. While the officials may start the engine for you, a test drive is out of the question. Crawling under and around the car as much as you want is permitted, but you can't suggest that the car you are interested in be jacked up, or attempt to do the job yourself. You can also ask to see any documentation available.

Bidding

Before you take part in the auction, **decide your maximum bid - and stick to it!**

It may take a while for the auctioneer to reach the lot you are interested in, so use that time to observe how other bidders behave. When it's the turn of your car, attract the auctioneer's attention and make an early bid. The auctioneer will then look to you for a reaction every time another bid is made, usually the bids will be in fixed increments until the bidding slows, whereupon smaller increments will often be accepted before the hammer falls. If you want to withdraw from the bidding, make sure the auctioneer understands your intentions - a vigorous shake of the head when he or she looks to you for the next bid should do the trick!

Assuming that you are the successful bidder, the auctioneer will note your card or paddle number, and from that moment on you will be responsible for the vehicle.

If the car is unsold, either because it failed to reach the reserve or because there was little interest, it may be possible to negotiate with the owner, via the auctioneers, after the sale is over.

Successful bid

There are two more items to think about. How to get the car home, and insurance. If you can't drive the car, your own or a hired trailer is one way, another is to have the vehicle shipped using the facilities of a local company. The auction house will also have details of companies specialising in the transfer of cars.

Insurance for immediate cover can usually be purchased on site, but it may be more cost-effective to make arrangements with your own insurance company in advance, and then call to confirm the full details.

Note for eBay bidders. Be aware that some cars offered for sale are ghost cars. **Don't** part with **any** cash without being sure that the vehicle does actually exist and is as described (usually pre-bidding inspection is possible).

11 Paperwork
– correct documentation is essential!

The paper trail

Classic, collector and prestige cars usually come with a large portfolio of paperwork accumulated and passed on by a succession of proud owners. This documentation represents the real history of the car and from it can be deduced the level of care the car has received, how much it's been used, which specialists have worked on it and the dates of major repairs and restorations. All of this information will be priceless to you as the new owner, so be very wary of cars with little paperwork to support their claimed history.

Registration documents

All countries/states have some form of registration for private vehicles whether its like the American 'pink slip' system or the British 'log book' system.

It is essential to check that the registration document is genuine, that it relates to the car in question, and that all the vehicle's details are correctly recorded, including chassis/VIN and engine numbers (if these are shown). If you are buying from the previous owner, his or her name and address will be recorded in the document: this will not be the case if you are buying from a dealer.

In the UK the current (Euro-aligned) registration document is named "V5C", and is printed in coloured sections of blue, green and pink. The blue section relates to the car specification, the green section has details of the new owner and the pink section is sent to the DVLA in the UK when the car is sold. A small section in yellow deals with selling the car within the motor trade.

In the UK the DVLA will provide details of earlier keepers of the vehicle upon payment of a small fee, and much can be learned in this way.

If the car has a foreign registration there may be expensive and time-consuming formalities to complete. Do you really want the hassle?

Roadworthiness certificate

Most country/state administrations require that vehicles are regularly tested to prove that they are safe to use on the public highway and do not produce excessive emissions. In the UK that test (the 'MoT') is carried out at approved testing stations, for a fee. In the USA the requirement varies, but most states insist on an emissions test every two years as a minimum, while the police are charged with pulling over unsafe-looking vehicles.

In the UK the test is required on an annual basis once a vehicle becomes three years old. Of particular relevance for older cars is that the certificate issued includes the mileage reading recorded at the test date and, therefore, becomes an independent record of that car's history. Ask the seller if previous certificates are available. Without an MoT the vehicle should be trailored to its new home, unless you insist that a valid MoT is part of the deal. (Not such a bad idea this, as at least you will know the car was roadworthy on the day it was tested and you don't need to wait for the old certificate to expire before having the test done.)

Road licence

The administration of every country/state charges some kind of tax for the use of its road system, the actual form of the 'road licence' and, how it is displayed, varying enormously country to country and state to state.

Whatever the form of the 'road licence', it must relate to the vehicle carrying it and must be present and valid if the car is to be driven on the public highway legally. The value of the license will depend on the length of time it will continue to be valid.

In the UK if a car is untaxed because it has not been used for a period of time, the owner has to inform the licencing authorities, otherwise the vehicle's date-related registration number will be lost and there will be a painful amount of paperwork to get it re-registered. Also in the UK, vehicles built before the end of 1972 are provided with 'tax discs' free of charge, but they must still display a valid disc. Car clubs can often provide formal proof that a particular car qualifies for this valuable concession.

Certificates of authenticity

For many makes of collectible car it is possible to get a certificate proving the age and authenticity (*e.g.* engine and chassis numbers, paint colour and trim) of a particular vehicle, these are sometimes called 'Heritage Certificates' and if the car comes with one of these it is a definite bonus. If you want to obtain one, the relevant owners club is the best starting point.

If the car has been used in European classic car rallies it may have a FIVA (*Federation Internationale des Vehicules Anciens*) certificate. The so-called 'FIVA Passport', or 'FIVA Vehicle Identity Card,' enables organisers and participants to recognise whether or not a particular vehicle is suitable for individual events. If you want to obtain such a certificate go to <www.fbhvc.co.uk> or <www.fiva.org> there will be similar organisations in other countries too.

Valuation certificate

Hopefully, the vendor will have a recent valuation certificate, or letter signed by a recognised expert stating how much he, or she, believes the particular car to be worth (such documents, together with photos, are usually needed to get 'agreed value' insurance). Generally such documents should act only as confirmation of your own assessment of the car rather than a guarantee of value as the expert has probably not seen the car in the flesh. The easiest way to find out how to obtain a formal valuation is to contact the owners club.

Service history

Often these cars will have been serviced at home by enthusiastic (and hopefully capable) owners for a good number of years. Nevertheless, try to obtain as much service history and other paperwork pertaining to the car as you can. Naturally, dealer stamps, or specialist garage receipts score most points in the value stakes. However, anything helps in the great authenticity game, items like the original bill of sale, handbook, parts invoices and repair bills, adding to the story and the character of the car. Even a brochure correct to the year of the car's manufacture is a useful document and something that you could well have to search hard to locate in future years. If the seller claims that the car has been restored, then expect receipts and other evidence from a specialist restorer.

If the seller claims to have carried out regular servicing, ask what work was completed, when, and seek some evidence of it being carried out. Your assessment of the car's overall condition should tell you whether the seller's claims are genuine.

Restoration photographs

If the seller tells you that the car has been restored, then expect to be shown a series of photographs taken while the restoration was under way. Pictures taken at various stages, and from various angles, should help you gauge the thoroughness of the work. If you buy the car, ask if you can have all the photographs as they form an important part of the vehicle's history. It's surprising how many sellers are happy to part with their car and accept your cash, but want to hang on to their photographs! In the latter event, you may be able to persuade the vendor to get a set of copies made.

12 What's it worth to you?
– be realistic, head over heart!

Chapter 9 has given you an assesment of the car's condition, but it's worth repeating that the older/rarer the Beetle the more likely it is to warrant decent money to purchase it and additional spending to bring it up to condition.

A basket case Hebmuller (an extremely rare two-seater coupé-version of the Beetle) would be worth snapping up even if the same price would buy you a fully-restored, low mileage sixties example. A 1967 1500 Beetle that has seen better days might be worth restoring if the asking price is suitably low, but forget the basket case 1303. The newer the car, the more 'excellent scores', or at least 'good ratings' there need to be!

The cheapest model during the fifties, the Standard, is likely to command more than an equivalent Deluxe today, thanks to its comparative rarity. On the other hand, the relatively rare semi-automatic, launched in 1968, would probably be avoided by most due to its poor reputation and the likelihood of costly repairs.

As a vehicle designed for economy motoring, factory-fitted extras are few and far between. The packages dreamed up by VW for the limited edition models of the seventies might add a little to the value. Genuine or acknowledged bolt-on accessories from the fifties and sixties are worth money. Even a period radio would come into this category, while a Judson Supercharger would be out of this world to many! Modern accessories can be voted down from the start. If the door cards have been damaged by the insertion of speakers for a radio and CD player, something that could well mean damage to the dash as well, the price offered for the car should fall accordingly.

All of this leads us nicely into customising. Buying and selling such vehicles is a minefield. Whiz wheels, lowered suspension, engine conversions involving cutting chunks out of the bodywork, plus filler to accommodate a smoothed out dashboard and removal of the car's original trim, not to mention the wildest of funky paintwork colours, are all very much a matter of personal preference. One thing is certain; if you spend a lot of money on a bog-standard Beetle, you're extremely unlikely to recoup the outgoings when you come to re-sell. So, if you opt to buy a customised Beetle, expect to be asked to pay a premium price, but offer less, much less, if you wish to break even in the long term.

Just because you don't think you're good enough at bargaining with someone don't be deterred. After all, if you fail dismally and you really want the car, the original asking price will still be there to be paid. However, having digested this guide you should be in a position not only to know what the car's potential faults are, but also how much it will cost to rectify them. Remember that even straightforward items are open to negotiation. A set of tyres that have enough tread left on them to keep them legal, but nevertheless will need replacing within six months, must justify a discount of at least 50% of the price it will actually cost to replace them. A dealer, while inevitably out to make as much for his business as possible, will be open to negotiation if the car you are after has been on the books for a while.

13 Do you really want to restore?

– it'll take longer and cost more than you think ...

The biggest cost of any restoration project put into the hands of professionals is not the parts you'll need, or the materials involved, but labour. Such restorations don't come cheap, and there are three other issues to consider when dealing with the trade.

First, make it abundantly clear what you want doing. It's no use simply indicating that the car needs to be restored. For example, are all replacement panels to be new old stock, or at least correct for the year? Is a respray to be a bare metal one? Should all window glass be removed prior to painting? The list is endless if you are going to be fair to the professionals and if, in turn, they are to give you the result required. Changing plans as you go along will cost you a small fortune.

Secondly, make sure that not only is a detailed estimate involved, but also that it is binding. We've all heard the stories of a person quoted one figure only to be presented with an invoice for a far larger one!

Thirdly, check that the company you're dealing with has a good reputation. The work of some well-

1968 semi-automatic 1500, probably worth ●x100 ... parts sold separately could raise about ●x500!

known companies has proved disappointing: you don't want to be faced with the prospect of having the car restored for a second time.

Restoring a car yourself requires a number of skills which, if you already have them, is marvellous, but acquiring the same might not be an overnight process. Can you weld, can you prepare and spray a car; can you rebuild an engine, and have you got the equipment and the workspace? Of course, you might elect to oversee the project but have you sufficient friends/contacts with the expertise to accomplish all you require? Above all, have your contacts got time to do the jobs you want according to the schedule you set?

Be prepared for a top-notch professional to put you on a lengthy waiting list or, if tackling a restoration yourself, expect things to go wrong and set aside extra time to complete the task. We can think of folks who have taken over two years to restore what wasn't an absolute basket case, and at least one other who pushed things

To fix this car you would need new floorpan halves, heater channels and adjacent panels – not to mention the services of a good upholsterer.

through in well under a year ... but at the cost of his marriage!

Some go for a rolling restoration, but if concours is the goal, that's not a good idea. In the UK, all year usage with panels still in primer will result in severe deterioration due to the salt of an average winter. The biggest danger of all with either rolling restorations, or hobby-based projects, is loss of interest, as either the project drags out, or the icy garage becomes less and less hospitable! How many cars do you see advertised as 'unfinished projects'? Part-finished cars inevitably spell financial loss, and many can be quite difficult to move on.

Do it yourself and it might cost c.⬤x1000 to get it roadworthy, plus whatever you want to pay for a respray. Might be worth it, for a relatively rare model ...

1974 1303 S Limited Edition Big Beetle. Most people wouldn't consider restoring a 1303, but this car might be worth it as it's a limited edition. Worst case scenario, rescue the wheels ... they are 5½ J sports wheels ... hen's teeth type!

14 Paint problems
– a bad complexion, including dimples, pimples and bubbles ...

Orange peel
This effect, where the paint surface looks like the skin of an orange, is caused by excess paint and, together with cracking and peeling paint surfaces, will indicate that the car has already undergone repairs and a partial or full respray. Rubbing down with very fine grades of abrasive paper can resolve the problem sometimes: consult a paint shop for advice.

Fading
Fading paint colours can be caused by sunlight, especially if a car lacks polish protection. Poor quality retouching can also be at the root of this problem. Proprietary paint restorers and paint cutting compounds will retrieve all but the worst cases.

Blistering/bubbling
Bubbling paint on steel panels indicates corrosion that has already perforated the metal. The corrosion will always be more extensive than the paint damage indicates.

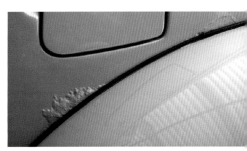

Blistering is caused, in this instance, by creeping rust underneath the wing (fender) piping.

Micro blistering
Often the result of an economy respray where inadequate heating has allowed moisture to settle on the car before spraying. Also caused by car covers that don't 'breathe'. Consult a paint specialist, though damaged paint will usually have to be removed before partial or full respraying.

'Pimples' of rust originating from dampness in the respray process, or rust on a panel before paint application.

Peeling
Often a problem with metallic paintwork when the sealing lacquer becomes damaged and begins to peel off. Poorly applied paint may also peel.

Cracking
Severe cases are likely to have been

The lacquer is peeling, causing problems for the paint beneath.

caused by too heavy an application of paint (or filler beneath the paint). Also, insufficient stirring of the paint before application can mean components are improperly mixed, and cracking can result. Incompatibility with the paint already on the panel can have a similar effect. To rectify the problem it's necessary to rub down to a smooth, sound finish before respraying the problem area.

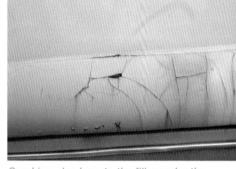

Cracking, due here to the filler under the paint lifting.

Crazing
Sometimes the paint takes on a crazed rather than a cracked appearance when the problems mentioned under 'Cracking' are present. This problem can also be caused by a reaction between the underlying and surface paints. Paint removal and respraying the problem area is usually the only solution.

Dimples
Dimples in the paintwork are caused by the residue of polish (particularly silicone types) not being removed properly before respraying. Paint removal and repainting is the only solution.

Dents
Small dents are usually easily cured by the 'Dentmaster', or equivalent process, that sucks or pushes out the dent, as long as the paint surface is still intact. Companies offering dent removal services usually come to your home: consult your telephone directory.

15 Lack of use problems
– just like their owners, cars need exercise!

Hydraulic problems caused by water in brake fluid

Brake fluid is hydroscopic (it absorbs water) and, if left unused for long periods, affects braking performance, which manifests itself as a spongy feel to the brake pedal. It also lowers the boiling point of the fluid, which considerably reduces braking performance and can even cause complete failure.

Silt in crankcase

Check the oil on the dipstick. If the engine has not run for some time, it's likely that the carbon and sludge that was suspended in the oil has now settled as a black acidic deposit on all internal surfaces. This can usually be sorted with an oil change, followed by another after 500 gently driven miles. In a worst case scenario, the acid in the oil could have attacked the crankshaft and other engine bearings, resulting in trouble further down the line.

Flatted tyres

It's likely that a car which has stood unused for a long period will have flat, or semi-flat, tyres which have been pumped up in an attempt to resurrect them. Tread flatting will manifest itself as a thumping noise on each revolution of the affected wheel. As tyres have a finite life of three to four years, if there are any doubts regarding their safety, such as cracks in the sidewalls, they should be changed at the earliest opportunity.

Shock absorbers (dampers)

Until April 1951, lever arm shock absorbers were fitted to the rear; all later cars are fitted with the telescopic type. Cars that have been idle for some time often suffer from seal breakdown, resulting in fluid loss. They can also seize completely. Visually check each shock absorber for fluid loss and then press down on each corner of the car to check efficiency. When released the car should return to normal ride height without bouncing further. Malfunction of either test would result in a failure of the official roadworthiness test. Apart from the foregoing, Volkswagen shock absorbers give a long service life.

Rubber and plastics cracking and losing elasticity

Due to the age of the cars, most have had their body rubber seals replaced, often with inferior copies of South American origin. These, particularly the boot (trunk) and engine cover seals, deteriorate very badly. Window seals also fail in a similar

Perished window seals often conceal frame rust due to water ingress.

way, resulting in water entering the car. Beetles that have been standing often have green mould and lichen growing on the window seals, which hastens their demise. Door seals harden with age, allowing the ingress of water. Engine and cooling system seals can also fail after prolonged periods of idleness. Wiper blades will harden over time too.

Corroded electrical connections

Expect some electrical circuits to fail on a car that has been idle. This is often due to corrosion on the ends of the ceramic continental fuses, which can be cleaned with fine-grain emery paper. Most circuits use 6.3mm spade connectors, which can be cleaned in the same way to maintain peak efficiency and avoid voltage drops, particularly on 6-volt cars.

Rotting exhaust system

Expect to replace the exhaust system on any Beetle which has stood idle for 6 months or more.

Tyres that have been flat for some time will need replacing, due to irreparable damage to the sidewalls.

A rotten exhaust isn't a problem as it's cheap to replace!

16 The Community
– key people, organisations and companies in the world of the Beetle

Auctioneers
Barrett-Jackson
www.barrett-jackson.com
Bonhams
www.bonhams.com
British Car Auctions BCA)
www.bca-europe.com
www.british-car-auctions.co.uk
Cheffins
www.cheffins.co.uk
Christies
www.christies.com
Coys
www.coys.co.uk
eBay
www.ebay.com
H&H
www.classic-auctions.co.uk
RM
www.rmauctions.com
Shannons
www.shannons.com.au
Silver
www.silverauctions.com

UK clubs
Here are some of the key UK
players, (details correct at the time of
publication) -
Historic Volkswagen Owners Club
c/o 28 Longnor Road, Telford,
Shropshire, TF1 3NY
Tel 01952 242167
www.historicvws.org.uk
**The Mexican and Brazilian Beetle
Register**
c/o 24 Green Acres, Ludlow,
Shropshire, SY8 1LU.
Tel 01584 872186
VW Cabriolet Owners Club GB
c/o 6,Station Road, Verwood, Dorset,
BH31 7PU. Tel 01202 820093

www.beetlecabrio.co.uk
**Volkswagen Owners Club (Great
Britain) - for owners of all ages of
Beetle and other VWs**
c/o PO Box 7, Burntwood, Staffs, WS7
2SB. Tel 01952 242167
www.vwocgb.com

European clubs
Netherlands
Kever Club Nederland (KCN)
www.keverclub.nl
Email: info@keverclub.nl
**Luchtgekoelde VW Club Nederland
(LVWCN)**
www.lvwcn.nl
Email: info@lvwcn.nl
Austria
DKT - Der Kleine Torpedo
Hugogasse 18/10, 1110 Wien, Austria
Contact: Earnst Bernsteiner
Tel: 0043 664 411 9822
Email: dkt@aon.at
www.derkleinetorpedo.com
Belgium
BBT - www.bbt4vw.com
Der Benzin Sa fers (DBS)
Contact: Goffaux Sven
Neerrechemstraat 60, 9770 Kruishoutem
Belgium, Tel: 0032475920918
Email: Gimini71@pandora.be
**Raouls VW Hallen Limburgse VW
Hobbyclub vzw**
Contact: Raoul Verbeemen
Email raouls.vw.hallen@skynet.be
Tel: 0032 475 958905
Fax: 0032 115 91158
www.raoulsvwhallen.com
Denmark
Copenhagen Wings
Nick Moberg, Brohusgade 11, 4.th.
DK-2200 Copenhagen N, Denmark

Email: admin@copenhagenwings.dk
www.copenhagenwings.dk

Finland

Die Wolfgranze Luftwaffe
Raivaajantie 9, 80160 Joensuu, Finland
Contact: Jari Tolvanen
Email: dwl@dwl.fi
Tel: 00358 505 387454
Fax: 00358 131 481505
www.dwl.fi

Finnish Volkswagen Association FVWA
PL 1, 33581 TAMPERE
Contact: Jani Antikainen
Email: puheenjohtaja@fvwa.fi
Tel: 00358 503 033866

France

Dream Machine
www.dreammachine.fr
VW Parts - www.vwparts.fr

Germany

Custom & Speed Parts
www.customspeedparts.de
Der Fieser Luftkühlers VW Club
Astsernweg 16, 38446 Wolfsburg,
Germany, Contact: Tobias Pleines
Tel: 0049 (0) 179 3887758
Email: DFL_VWClub@hotmail.com
Piranha VW & Audi Club
Contact: Jens Dommes
Email: PiranhaGermany@aol.com
Tel: 0049 (0) 175 2711465
Volkswagen Team Frankfurt
Contact: Juergen Amberg
Talaeckerst 21, 65933 Frankfurt,
Email: vwamberg@aol.com
Tel: 0049 177 451 2130
VW Boxer Club Gettingen e.V.
Contact: Thomas Moebes
Rosmarinweg 37, 37081 Gettingen
Tel: 0049 551 62646
Email: Thomas-moebes@vwboxerclub.de
www.vwboxerclub.de
VW Club Rhein Neckar
Contact: George Maas
Starke Hoffnung 28, 68305 Mannheim,

Email: georg@vwclub-rheinneckar.de
Tel: 0049 621 745593
Fax: 0049 621 853805
www.vwclub-rheinneckar.de

Norway

Folkevognklubben Cool Cruisers
PO Box 434 1601 Fredrikstad, Norway
Email: info@folkevognklubben.no
www.folkevognklubben.no

Portugal

Fanaticos do Carocha
Rua Francisco Marques Beato 58, 1885
031 Moscavide, Portugal
Contact: Pedro Silva Reis
Tel: 0035 121944 3348
Email: fanaticocarocha@netcabo.pt
www.netclassicos.com/fanaticos.
do.carocha

Russia

V-Dub Dialogue
Website: www.vdubdialogue.da.ru
The online Russian VW club

Spain

Amics del Volkswagen de Catalunya
Apt. 14.124 08080 Barcelona, Catalonia,
Contact: Marcel Olsina
Tel: 00 34 93 304 0393
Fax: 0034 93 412 2103
Email: avwc@hotmail.com
www.geocities.com/avwc_escarabajo

Sweden

Beirut Buggers
Contact: Klas Adolf
Tel: 0046 704053470
Email: vwtyp3@hotmail.com
VW club from south Stockholm
Stockholm V-dubs
Contact:Kjell Ostlund
c/o Sederlin Skolvagen 11, 141 44
Huddinge
Tel: 08-600 0473 or 070-767 4525
Email: stockholm@v-dubs.com
Biggest VW-club in Stockholm
VW-Airheads
Lagmansgatan 7D, 46237 Vanersborg,

Sweden
Contact: Jan Sandin
Email: info@vwairheads.org
Tel: 004652118476
www.vwairheads.org

Switzerland
GEZUVOR VW Club
Contact: Marc Woeltinger
Diebold-Schillingstrasse 24
CH-6004 Lucerne, Switzerland
www.gezuvor.ch

US clubs
Vintage Volkswagen Club of America
Russell Cordell
Email: membership@vvwca.com
1441 Forest St.
Springdale, AR 72764
Tel: 001 479 750 2328 or 750 6380
www.vvwca.com

Deutsch Akzent Alte Schule Volkswagens
13247 Blodgett Ave, Downey CA 90242
Contact: Kai Eastburn
Tel: 562-634-4690

The German Folks
10512 Kibbee Avenue, Whittier, California 90603
Contact: John Canales
Tel: 001 562 902 9465
Mobile: 001 562 665 6840
Email: thegermanfolks@aol.com

Harsh Winters Vintage VW Club
Contact: Joe Hauge II; c/o HWVVC, 1117 Douglas Avenue, Aurora IL 60505
Tel: 001 (630) 896-2449
EMail: hwvvc@hotmail.com

Kustom Wagen VW Club
Downey, California
Contact: Marco Rivera
Tel: 001 562 773-5873
Email: crazy69bug@netzero.net

Las Vegas VW Club
Contact: Scott Faivre

2627 Cactus Hill Drive, Las Vegas
Email: scott@lasvegasvwclub.com
www.lasvegasvwclub.com
An officially licensed VW club

North Eastern Volkswagen Association
PO Box 84, Massapequa Park, New York, NY 11762
Contact: Glenn Ring
Tel: 001 516 799 4395
Email: NEVA@glenn-ring.com

Portland Air Coolers
Contact: Chris Spinks
15284 SW Royalty C-28, Tigard, OR 97224
Email: gijoe101st@portlandaircoolers.com
www.portlandaircoolers.com
Tel: 001 503 620 7009

Southern Oregon Volkswagen Club
South Oregon
Contact: Garry Henry
Tel: 001 541 261 3466
www.sovw.com

Super Beetles only
Los Angeles, California
Email: info@superbeetlesonly.com
www.superbeetlesonly.com

Worldwide clubs
Australia
Klub VW Bayside
14 Soiandra St, Birkdale, Queensland 4159
Contact: Moniek or Michael Hoffmann
Email: klub_vw_bayside@yahoo.com
Tel: 0061 (07)38248997

Volks Enthusiasts Club SA Inc
Contact: David O'Connor; PO Box 306, Kent Town, South Australia, 5071
Tel: 0061 618-8271-9103
Email: volksenthusiasts@charior.net.au

New Zealand
Volkswagen Owners Club
Contact: John Atkinson
PO BOX 12-538, Penrose, Auckland,

Tel: 0064 9 8325824
Email: jrwa@clear.net.nz

European specialists
Here are some of the well known names. Our listing does not imply recommendation and is not deemed to be comprehensive.
VW Heritage Parts Centre (parts)
Hollands Lane, Henfield, West Sussex, BN5 9QY. Tel 01273 495800
www.vwheritage.com
Karmann Konnection (parts and some car sales)
6 Grainger Road, Southend on Sea
Tel 01702 601155
www.karmannkonnection.com
German Swedish & French (parts)
Branches all over the country. Mail order 020 8917 3866.
www.gsfcarparts.com
Beetlelink (servicing, restoration and sales)
Units DI & D2, Preymead Farm, Badshot Lea, Farnham, Surrey, GU9 9LR.
Tel 01252 326767
www.beetlelink.co.uk
Henley Beetles (VW Beetles re-built to order)
Northfield Road, Lower Shiplake, Henley on Thames, Oxon, RG9 3PA.
Tel 01189 403464
www.henleybeetles.co.uk
www.rccimport.co.uk (Beetle sales and imported parts)
Rhiwlas Farm. Llanbedr, Ruthin, North Wales, LL15 1US. Tel 01824 702768
Volksheaven (VW salvage)
Tel 01302 351355
www.volksheaven.co.uk
Volksgoods (electrical parts)
Tel 01522 751941
Laurie Ellis (rebuilt Solex carbs)
Tel 01724 720553
John Forbes (spares, service)
7 Meadow Lane, Edinburgh, EH8 9NR.

Tel 0131 667 9767
Cogbox (gearbox/transmission rebuilds and repairs)
London area. Tel 0208 842 2580
Richard Hulin (repairs and spares)
Gloucester. Tel 01452 502333
Stateside Tuning (engine machining and tuning specialist)
Moreton-in-Marsh, Glos
Tel 01608 812438
Mega-Bug (spares and salvage)
Unit 3, White Hart Road, Plumstead, SE18 1PG. Tel 0208 3177333
www.megabug.co.uk
Status VW (parts)
Tel 015242 72915
www.status-vw.co.uk

Worldwide specialists
These are just a few of the many VW specialists to be found in your area and/or on the internet.
Scat - www.scatvw.com (USA)
Wolfsburg West - www.wolfsburgwest.com (USA)
West Coast Metric - www.westcoastmetric.com (USA)
BFY Obsolete Parts - www.bfyobsoleteparts.com (USA)
Bill & Steve's - www.billandsteves.com (USA)
Vintage Parts Inc - www.vintagepartsinc.com (USA)
Koch's - www.kochs.com (USA)
Sewfine Interiors - www.sewfineproducts.com (USA)
Quality German Auto Parts - www.qualitygermanautoparts.com (USA)
Mid America Motorworks - www.mamotorworks.com (USA)
Bugzone - www.bugzone.net (USA)
Jbugs - www.jbugs.com (USA)
California Import Parts Ltd - www.cip1.com (USA)
Flat 4 - www.flat4.co.jp (Japan)

17 Vital statistics
- essential data at your fingertips

Number built -
21,529,464. With a production run as long as the Beetle's, inevitably there are many variations relating to most aspects of the car. We've picked three sample years for our glossary.

Performance -
1954 Deluxe - Max and cruising speed: 68mph 0-60: 34 seconds
1967 1500 - Max and cruising speed: 78mph, 0-60: 22.5 seconds
1973 1303S - Max and cruising speed: 81mph 0-60: 18.2 seconds

Engine -
1954 Deluxe - 4-cyl horizontally opposed air-cooled, 1192cc CR 6.1:1, 30bhp at 3400rpm
1967 1500 - As above, except 1493cc CR 7.5:1, 44bhp at 4000rpm
1973 1303S - As above, except 1584cc CR 8:1 50bhp at 4000rpm

Transmission
1954 Deluxe - Final drive ratio 4.4:1
1967 1500 - Final drive ratio 4.125:1
1973 1303S - Final drive ratio 3.875:1

Brakes
1954 Deluxe - Hydraulic - drums all round
1967 1500 - Hydraulic - discs up front (Not US models)
1973 1303S - Hydraulic - discs up front (Not US models)

Electrics
1954 Deluxe - 6-volt
1967 1500 - 6-volt (12-volt in US)
1973 1303S - 12-volt

Dimensions
1954 Deluxe - L - 13,194in/406.4cm, W - 5ft 1in/154.94cm, T 4ft 11in/149.86cm
1967 1500 - L 13,194½in/407.67cm, W - 5ft 1in/154.94cm, T - 4ft 11in/149.86cm
1973 1303S - L - 13,194½in (407.67cm), W - 5ft 2½in (158.75cm), T - 4ft 11¾in (151.76cm)

Weights
1954 Deluxe - Weight 14.2cwt
1967 1500 - Weight 15.7cwt
1973 1303S - Weight 16.9cwt

Matching engine and chassis number groups - German production

1954 Deluxe - Engine number 695 282, chassis number 575 415 (Jan 1st 1954).

1967 1500 - Engine number H 0874200, chassis number 117 000 001 (Aug 1st 1966).

1973 1303S - Engine number AD 0598 002 or AH 0 005 901, chassis number 133 2000 001 (Aug 1st 1972).

Major change points by date and, where applicable, chassis number

1949 July - Introduction of Export model, or Deluxe.

1950 April - Hydraulic brakes on Deluxe, 1-0158253.

1952 Oct - Dash redesigned, synchromesh on 2nd, 3rd & 4th (Deluxe only), plus many other changes, 1-0397 023.

1953 March - Introduction of oval shaped rear window, 1-0454951.

1953 Dec - Introduction of 30bhp engine (replacing 25bhp), 1-0575415.

1955 Aug - General revisions - identifiable by twin exhaust pipes, 1-0 929 746.

1957 Aug - New dash, much larger rear screen, 1 600 440.

1960 Aug - Engine uprated to 34bhp on Deluxe. Demise of the semaphore indicator! 3 192 507.

1961 Aug - All cars fitted with a fuel gauge at long last! 4 010 995.

1963 Aug - Replacement of fabric sunroof (introduced 1950) with crank-operated steel version, 5 677 119.

1964 Aug - All windows increased in size, 115 000001.

1965 Aug - Introduction of the 1285cc, 1.3 litre, 40bhp engine - the VW 1300 is born, 116 000001.

1966 Aug - Introduction of the 44bhp, 1493cc engine and the 1500 Beetle. Disc brakes up front (except US models), 117 000001.

1967 Aug - Introduction of the 'New Beetle' (at least according to the marketing men). Re-designed wings, boot and engine lid, square section bumpers - 12 volt electrics VW 1300 and VW 1500, 118 000001.

1970 Aug - Arrival of the 1302S Beetle, with MacPherson struts, 50bhp engine … a whole new breed of Beetle. Torsion bar models continue (except VW 1500), 1112000002.

1972 Aug - The 1303, a 1302 with a curved windscreen (windshield) makes its debut. Available widely as both a 1300 and a 1600 (known as the 1303S), 1332000004.

1976 July - At the end of the month all Beetles – other than the faithful old torsion bar 1200 and the cabriolet version of the 1303 (S) – are deleted from the range.

1978 Jan - On 19th January German Beetle production in saloon form comes to an end. Cars now imported from Mexico for sale in many European countries - but not GB. Cabriolet production continues until January 1980.

1985 Aug - Arrival last official Beetle consignment from Mexico - '50 year cars'.

1991 Jan - Mexican Beetles now have 1.6 litre carb engine + catalytic converter.

1993 Jan - Digifant fuel injection.

Also from Veloce Publishing –

ISBN - 1-903706-90-4 • £25.00

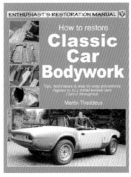

ISBN - 1-903706-62-9 • £17.99

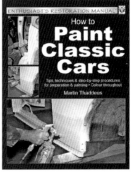

ISBN - 1-903706-63-7 • £13.99

ISBN - 1-903706-06-8 • £15.99

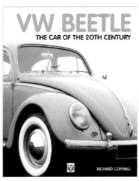

ISBN - 1-901295-86-9 • £29.99

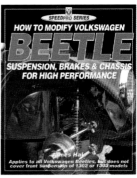

ISBN - 1-903706-99-8 • £17.99

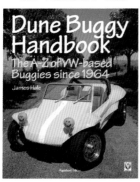

ISBN - 1-904788-21-1 • £19.99

ISBN - 1-903788-08-4 • £15.99

ISBN - 1-903706-93-9 • £19.99

For more details on these and other Veloce titles call 01305 260068
or visit our website:

www.veloce.co.uk

Index